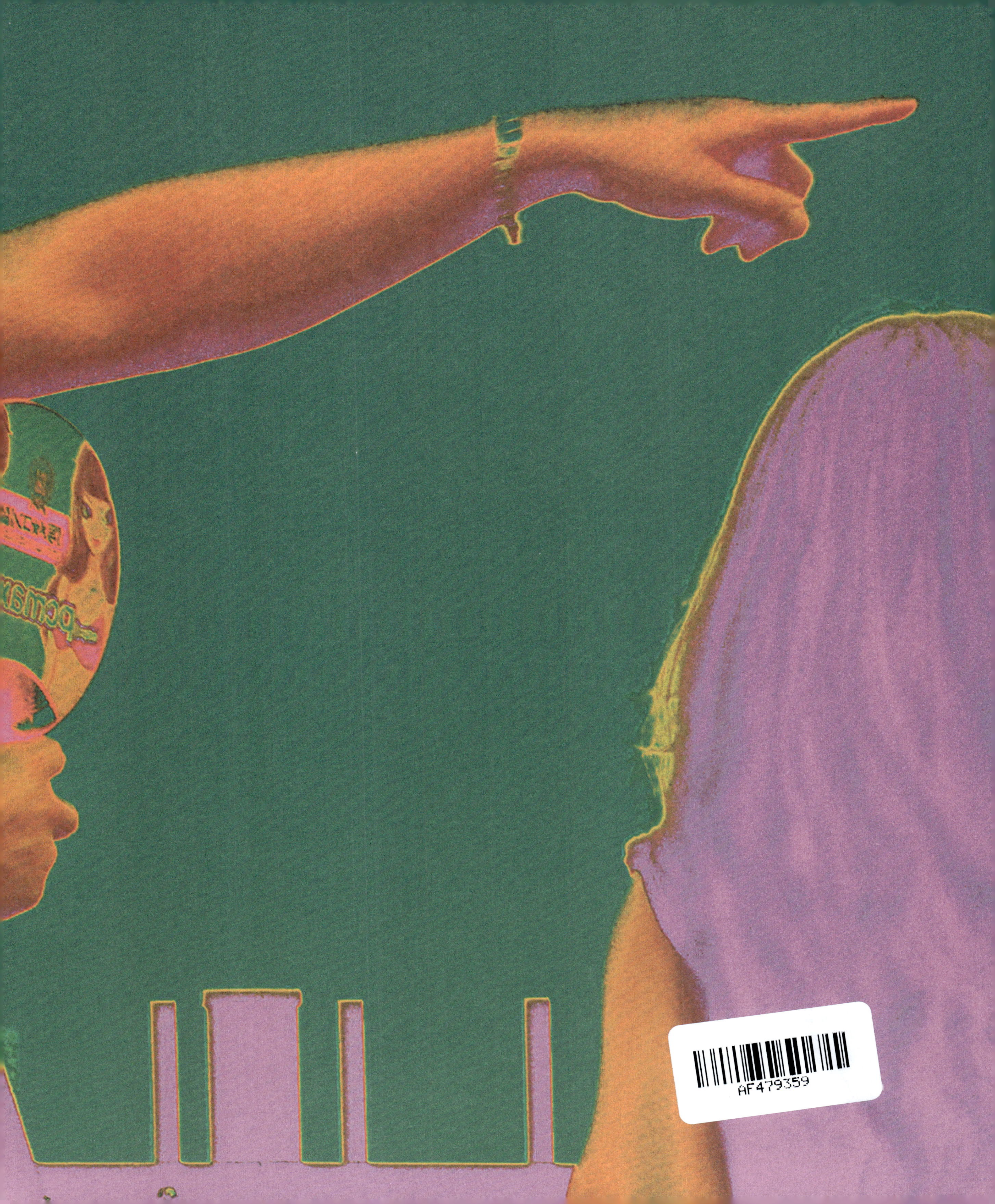
AF479359

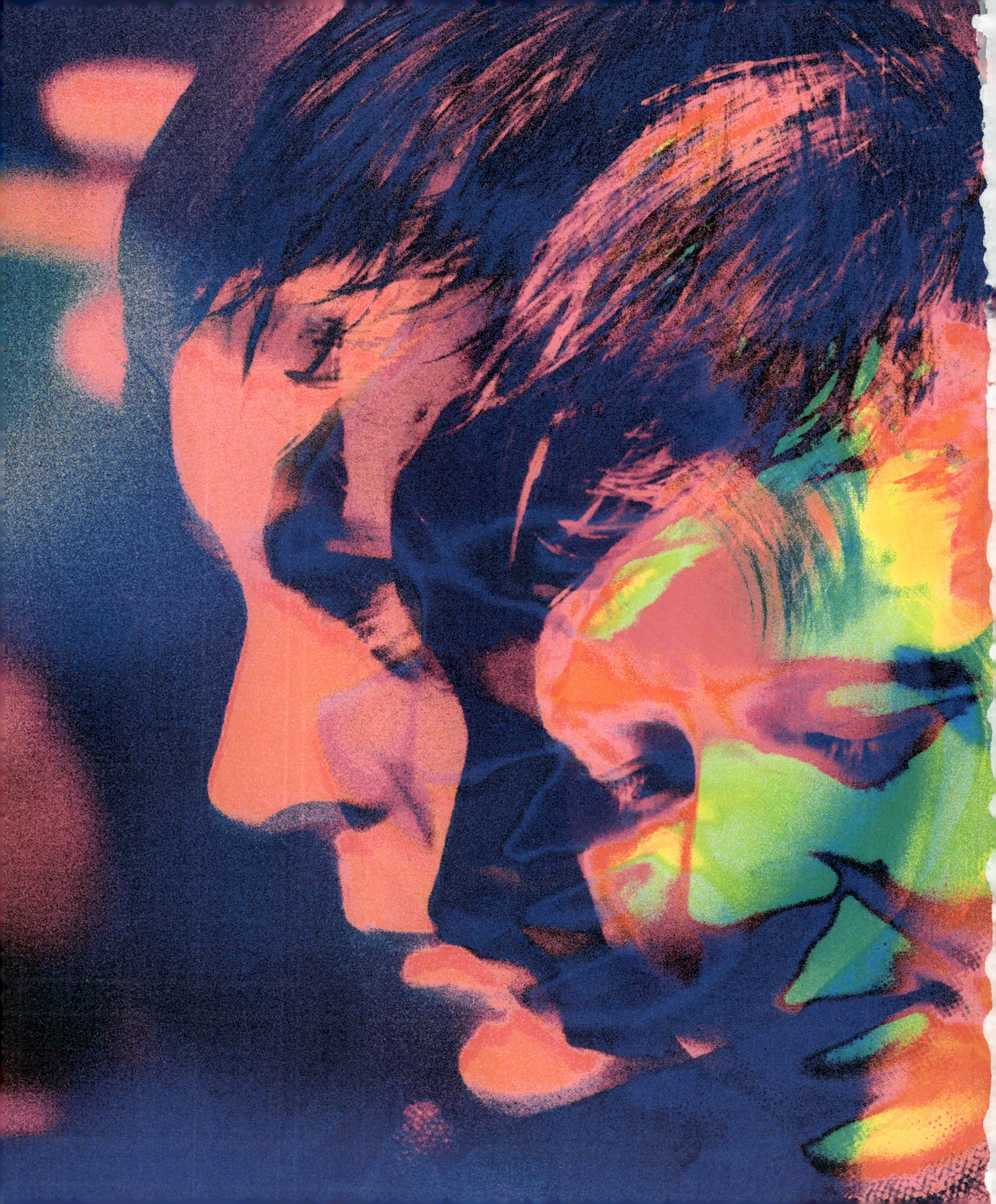

KLAUS MITTELDORF

N E X T

Contributions by Rubens Fernandes Junior and Joseph Akel

DAMIANI

Contents

To my my wife, Luisa, and my children, Otto, Max, and Luiza

Next: Complex Visualities

Rubens Fernandes Junior

The arts are not conceived as historically invariable actions of humankind, nor as an arsenal of "cultural goods" that live in a timeless existence, but rather as a process that unceasingly advances, as a "work in progress" in which every artwork participates.

—Hans Magnus Enzensberger

Next, a new series of images by São Paulo artist Klaus Mitteldorf, is unlike his first photo-essays, with their stunning syntheses of shapes wrought in an exuberance of striking colors, evincing the profound influence of his German origins on his visual production. They are also different from the pictures he made during his monochromatic forays, sometimes exploring the drama of black and white, sometimes navigating through the blues. He studied architecture and was a surfer along São Paulo's North Shore, where he made incredible experiments as a pioneering surf documentarist using Super-8 cinema; he has lived in Germany, created photographs for important national and international advertising campaigns, and worked as a fashion photographer and movie director.

Throughout his wide-ranging, successful career he has mastered various visual languages while transiting through a succession of mutually distinct phases, plotting new courses for his nearly always explosive, uneasy photography. Unbound from commercial restraints, his production is now graphically and artistically bolder than ever. This has garnered his work an unquestionable position of importance within the context of Brazilian photography of the last few decades.

Perhaps Mitteldorf's most noteworthy characteristic is the continuous flow of his production. In *Next*, the photographs—can we still call them photographs?—not only captivate our gaze but also throb in our retinas, making our central nervous system shift into high gear to unravel the visual puzzle it is faced with. I would say that it is nearly impossible to re-encounter the different times and places present in these pictures; when we can, it is through the help of clues provided by their titles. In the Western culture we are all immersed in, we always seek to discover the true meaning of what we see. It is hard to allow ourselves to be simply swept away by the beauty of the shapes or by the thrill of the signs that pulsate in each of these images.

When asked about them, Mitteldorf sidesteps: "I don't know how to explain it, but the first thing I knew, I was taken over by the need to create these images." They do not fit into any category or trend in contemporary photography. They synthesize this globalized world, where millions of devices and applications are available to all who wish to visually document their everyday life. In his visionary view, even though we see the images one by one, they "massage" our retina intermittently, as though they were superimposed on transparent, vibrating layers.

Canadian thinker Marshall McLuhan, who formed the precursor to the concept of the global village, stated that "there is absolutely no inevitability as long as there is a willingness to contemplate what is happening." This is precisely what Mitteldorf evidences in his images. In other words, in the not so distant future we will be seeing in a way predicted by the technological world, as though the visual possibilities allowed by technology anticipate what we may soon be seeing. McLuhan was also a pioneer in stating that each technological moment gives rise to a perceptually new man. It is enough to consider how sensorially different we are from our ancestors.

Certain historical shifts in visual language, of which we are already aware, can be associated with the images of the *Next* series. While the images foreshadow new perceptive possibilities, they also point to other moments of aesthetic rupture as a reference. *Next* inevitably brings to mind the experiments of Eadweard Muybridge, Étienne-Jules Marey, the Photodynamism of the Italian Futurists Giacomo Balla and the Bragaglia brothers, and even Cubism. In light of this visual vocabulary of movement, Mitteldorf proposes new visual configurations arising from his own explorations and elaborations other perceptive possibilities. The progress of art requires courage, boldness, and rebellion in order to create unlikely tensions and to counteract environmentally imposed visual patterns.

In 1967, Marcel Duchamp, in an interview given to critic Pierre Cabanne, stated that his greatest influence in making *Nude Descending a Staircase, No. 2* (1912) was not cinema, as many people had thought up to then. What had really touched him were Marey's pioneering experiments with chronophotography. Marey set forth the idea that photography could be more interesting if it did not seek to capture "the before" or "the after" of a given instant, but rather "the during" of the time span of a given action. This is an astonishing thought for those who still see photography as mere documental record of reality. Marey's research was so important and decisive for photographic language that it later paved the way for Duchamp's revolutionary ideas, which constituted a new paradigm for the visual arts.

Establishing paradigms in contemporaneity, independently from the media used, is nearly impossible. But artists unceasingly seek visual possibilities that record our own time or point to future paths. *Next* is a proposal that requires a perceptually differentiated spectator. It uses the same two-dimensional surface that has been central to photography for more than 170 years, including the experiments of Marey, of Photodynamism, and of Cubism, which sought to revoke the perspectivist illusion and to instate new modes of sensing and assimilating other sensations made possible by the technological world.

Mitteldorf has unveiled the essence of the contemporary world, centered on digital technology. The images acquire a Pop aspect that recalls some of Rauschenberg's collages from the 1960s. But of course beyond these possible references it is necessary to know about the artist, including his background and the procedures he uses. With know-how and perspicacity, Mitteldorf aims to question the photographic image, which for him was never the simple representation of reality.

His response is a radical one: he takes some of the technological effects and articulates them with the visual universe he has idealized in his creative paths. Mitteldorf proposes an interplay of images where blending, superposition, transparence, displacements, and other artifices trigger distinct sensations that intensify and prolong a supposed continuity of the photographic shot's frozen moment in time. He gives rise to a different sensation of rhythm that stems from the dynamic of the movements; he is concerned with the movement of a gesture; he explores the perception of the gaps between the movements. *Next* furthermore involves a performative character that is likewise present in other series the artist has produced, for example, *O Último Grito* (The Last Cry), where a performatory facet is discernible in the actions of the photographic subjects.

Now his photographs have taken on other visual characteristics, even while maintaining some of the unmistakable features of the aesthetics of his previous works, including color and movement, which accentuate their Pop character. Mitteldorf has always been impulsive in the construction of his images, whose complexity and provocative tone are enough to make the viewer question their veracity. But this is entirely consistent with his opposition to creating works with an unchangeable reality. *Next* unleashes a frenzied visual possibility without breaking away from a certain tradition, without aiming to be a disconcerting discovery; its original, authentic images come like a condemnation of the rampant imagistic banality of everyday life.

In his manifesto "Futurist Photodynamism" of 1911, Anton Giulio Bragaglia emphasizes that "we are certainly not concerned with the aims and characteristics of cinematography and chronophotography. We are not interested in the precise reconstruction of movement, which has already been broken up and analyzed. We are involved only in the area of movement which produces sensation, the memory of which still palpitates in our awareness." More than one hundred years later we come upon *Next*, the outcome of a free outlook that perceives the symbolic power of the layers that kindle the multiple sensations that pervade our gaze with transparencies and radiant visions of light. The interpenetrations and superpositions of the images evidence distinct times which nevertheless coexist in the elaborate, ethereal space created by Mitteldorf.

The rich visual experience proposed by the artist makes *Next* a look into the future, insofar as it tests our perceptions and proposes images in trance. It is simultaneously a look into the past, particularly into the sensations experienced by the Italian Futurists when they declared that "thanks to the persistence of the image on the retina, things in movement are multiplied, deformed, and follow each other like vibrations in the space they cross." This process of signs created on the basis of a prospective outlook is what makes the essay *Next* an innovative narrative in contemporary photography. It is the explicit wish to oppose an immutable reality.

Double, Vision

Joseph Akel

The photography of Klaus Mitteldorf defies easy categorization. In a career that now spans close to four decades, Mitteldorf's images would seem to subscribe to no one identifiable school, no one movement that might easily align him to an aesthetic tradition. Instead, the Brazilian-born photographer's work seems to chart a course that ebbs and flows with the interests and idiosyncrasies that capture his attention at the time. In the early 1970s, it was a fascination with the vibrant surf culture found along the glimmering azure shores of São Paulo and Rio de Janeiro, while the 80s heralded his growing stature in the realms of fashion and editorial photography, with his images regularly appearing in the likes of *Vogue Brasil* and *Claudia Moda*. By the conclusion of the first decade of 2000, Mitteldorf had some eight books to his name, along with numerous prizes and exhibitions. And yet, when you speak to Mitteldorf about his work, his legacy as a photographer, he is quick to note that each new body of work represents "a radical change in my life—the search for something wholly and utterly new." To that end, if there were to be a conceptual thread that tied his photography together over the years, it would likely be his ardent emphasis on reinvention and an unyielding, almost protean quality he brings to his aesthetic vision.

And so, for his project, aptly titled *Next*, Mitteldorf largely abandoned the visual language he had adopted in prior series such as *O Último Grito* or *Almaquatica*, adopting instead a compositional form marked equally by a playfulness of technique and a disruption of the photographic tropes of figuration. Indeed, throughout *Next*, one has the sense that Mitteldorf is reconsidering the medium of photography all over again, rethinking how to take photographs and, more importantly, what they should look like. In many ways, the images that comprise the series—the infinite urban grid of Tokyo, a candid portrait of a street crowded with pedestrians—made up of inverted exposures, double negatives, and skewed colors—are a means to "observe the world in a new way, with technology that allow us to do so."

Tellingly then, Mitteldorf's compositional and conceptual choices—the collocation of the bustling metropolis as a symbol of modernity's ensuing fractious state of being, combined with the candid, and ultimately distorted view of the individual within it—connects his work with the likes of both László Moholy-Nagy's New Vision movement and Man Ray and Maurice Tabard's Surrealist embrace of photography. One might go so far as to say that the curiosity and disregard for convention that Mitteldorf brings to the photographic medium echoes those held by the avant-garde artists at the turn of the last century, and importantly shares an ethos that locates within the technology of photography a means by which to reveal the deeper forces at work in our daily lives. To be sure, there are compositional similarities, especially with Mitteldorf's recurrent use of layered collage and the inversion of his digital negatives. But beyond the aesthetic, his images seemingly embrace a belief that is evocative of Moholy-Nagy's declaration in his seminal 1925 text, *Malerei, Photographie, Film* (Painting, Photography, Film) that photography is "a means of creation" rather than "a mechanical process of recording."

Indeed, for Moholy-Nagy, who was a leading figure in the Bauhaus-aligned New Vision movement, photography had the power to "transform human perception," and he stridently believed in unconventional, often technically groundbreaking approaches to its use. "Through formal and spatial connections," he writes in *Painting, Photography, Film*, "our eye completes the received optical phenomenon with our intellectual experience to create an image-concept [*Vorstellungsbild*], while the photographic apparatus reproduces the purely optical image and therefore shows recordings, distortions, shortenings, and so forth that are preserved in the optical."

And, when Moholy-Nagy and Siegfried Giedion were tasked with helping to curate the Deutscher Werkbund's historic 1929 FiFo exhibition (*Film und Foto*) in Stuttgart, they took it as an opportunity to showcase what they understood as photography's new technologically experimental, visually revelatory, direction. To be sure, when comparing images from Mitteldorf's *Next*, particularly his portraits, alongside Moholy-Nagy's photomontages, such as *Nude*, 1929, the compositional similarities are readily apparent. But, just as Mitteldorf embraces Moholy-Nagy's insistent technical kineticism, so to does he seemingly entertain the contingent, highly reflexive quality of photographic production that came to mark the works of the Surrealists.

As scholar Rosalind Krauss has noted in her 1981 essay "The Photographic Conditions of Surrealism," photography, far from being an eccentric element of the Surrealist movement was in fact "absolutely central" to it. So vital was the medium to the Surrealist enterprise that André Breton, the patriarch of the movement, included photography in three of his major works, *Nadja* (1928), *Les Vases communicants* (1932), and *L 'Amour fou* (1937), not to mention the vanguard periodical of the movement, *La Révolution surréalist*. Indeed, for the Surrealists, photography was one of the principle means through which to explore the human subconscious as well as an apt technology to more fully disrupt, and subsequently reflect upon, the condition of humanity in the burgeoning modern era. Among their favored techniques, photomontage was an approach they deployed to upend the status of the photograph as a mere marker of appearances, transforming the medium instead into a vehicle through which a hidden reality was laid bare.

In the case of Mitteldorf's *Next* series, we observe a similar approach to the production of his images, one that looks to deploy techniques that, through their visual disruption, gesture towards an alternate conception of the photographic image and its signification. For Mitteldorf, this is marked by a process that involves the use of photographic manipulation through computer software—layers are added to each other, their colors adjusted through an intuitive process that reflects a particular mood or emotional state. Speaking of his Dadaist photomontages from the 1920's, John Heartfeld noted, "a photograph can, by the addition of an unimportant spot of color, become a photomontage, a work of art of a special kind." The same could readily be true of Mitteldorf's images.

For Rosalind Krauss, central to the early avant-garde experimentation with photography was a belief in the medium's role as "operating as an extension of normal vision" one that, "supplements the deficiencies of the naked eye," functioning, she notes, "as a kind of prosthesis, enlarging the capacity of the human body." In the case of *Next*, we observe that Mitteldorf, in a similar fashion, seeks to use the photograph not only to portray reality anew, but in many ways to refashion it altogether. Far from an aesthetic conceit that merely adopts a visual discordance, Mitteldorf's images hope to reframe the very parameters by which we view world around us.

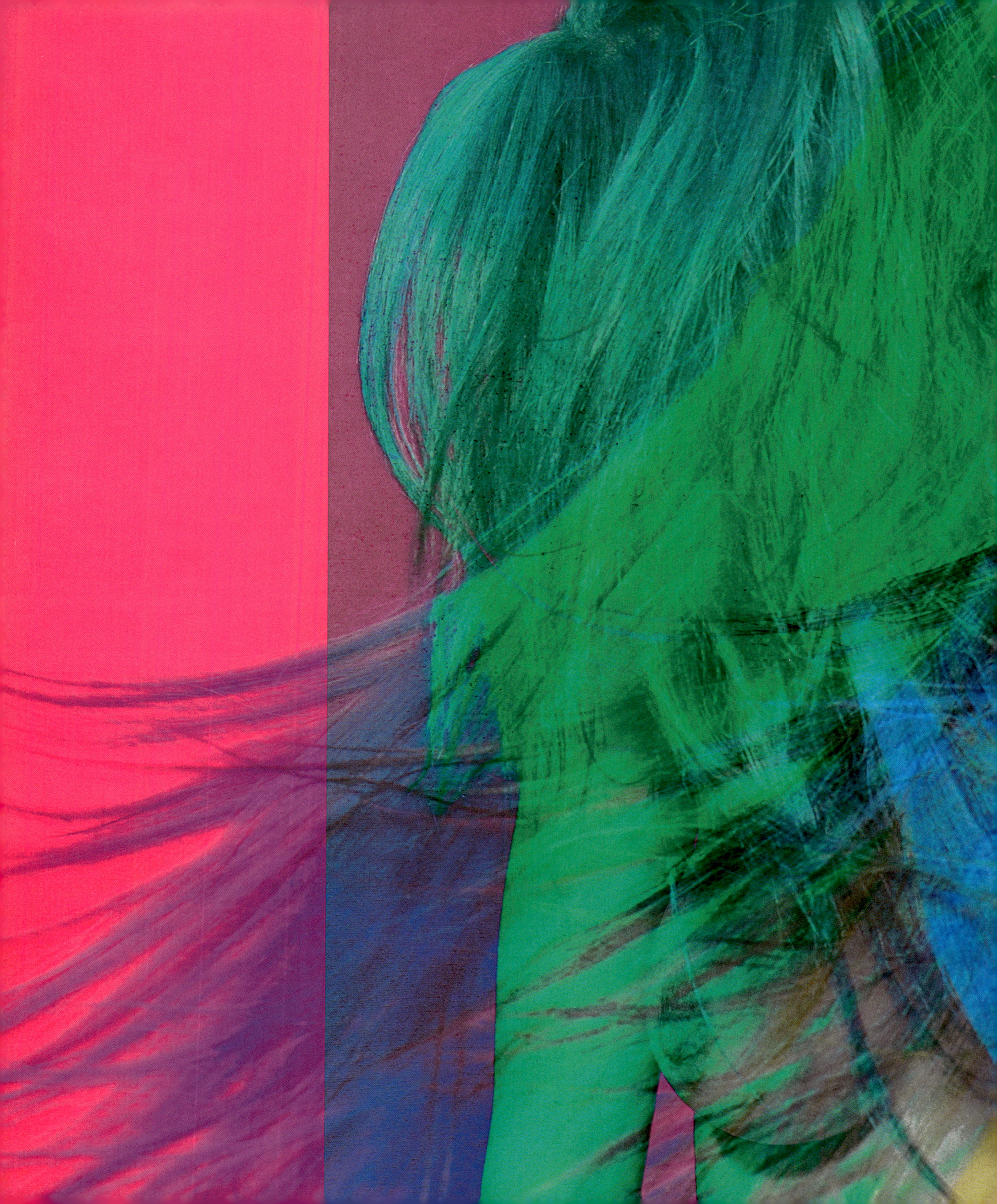

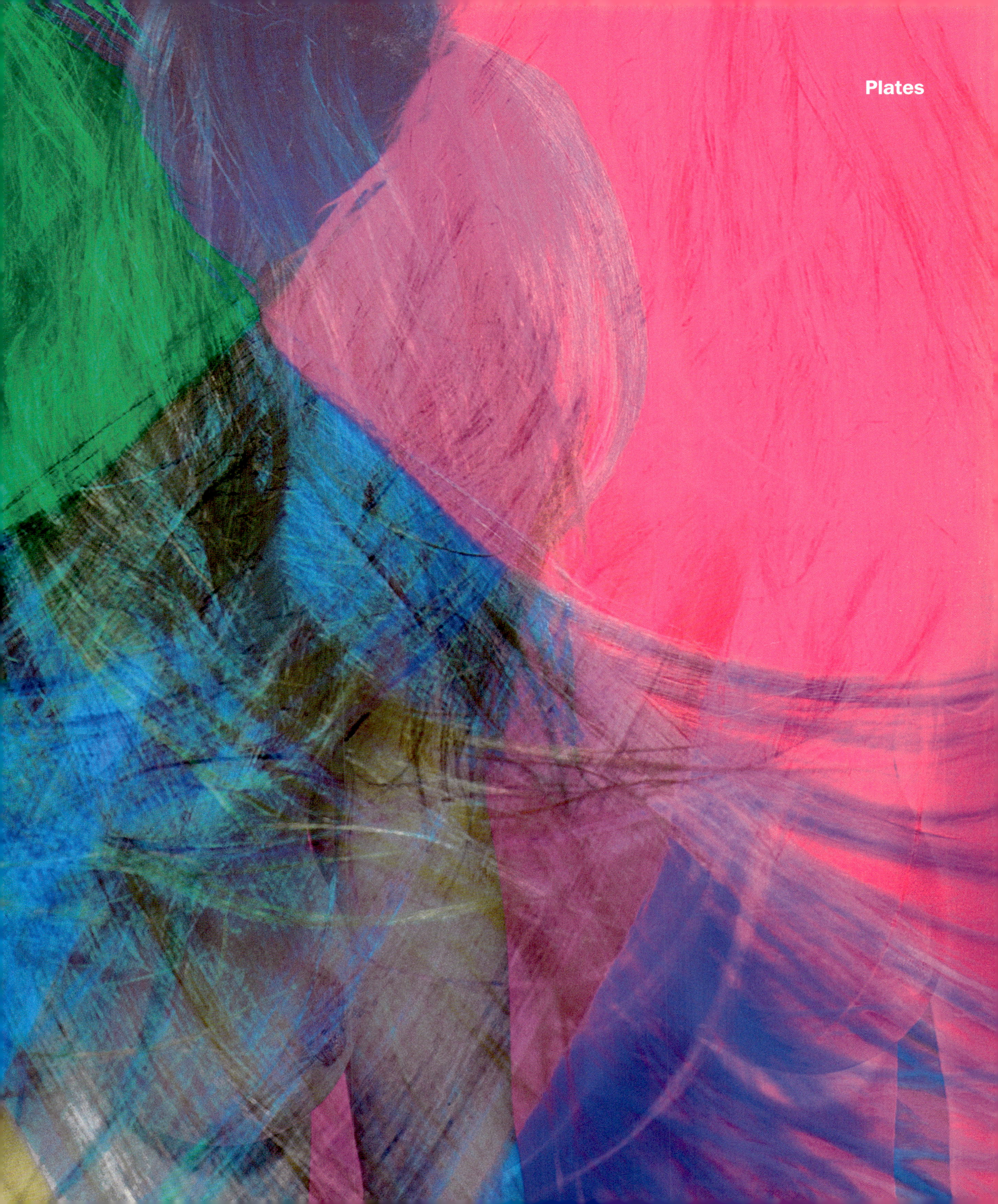
Plates

Berlin Face / Berlin / 2013

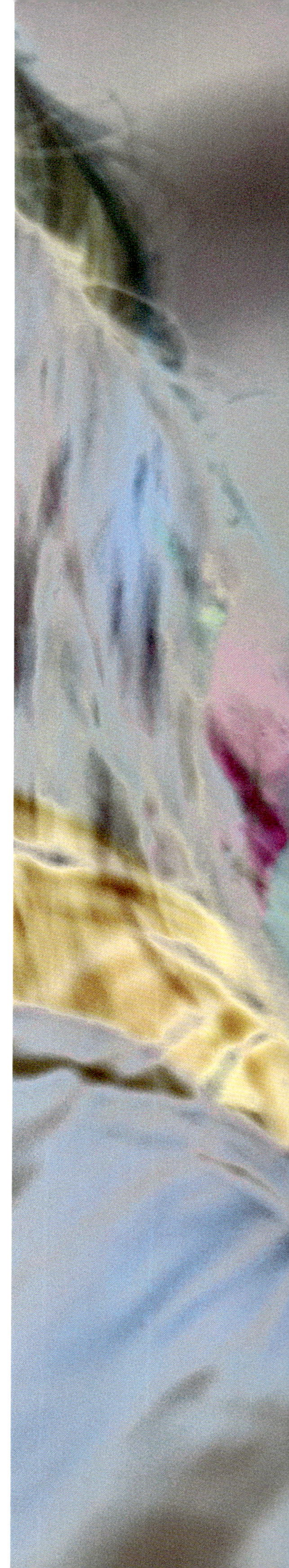

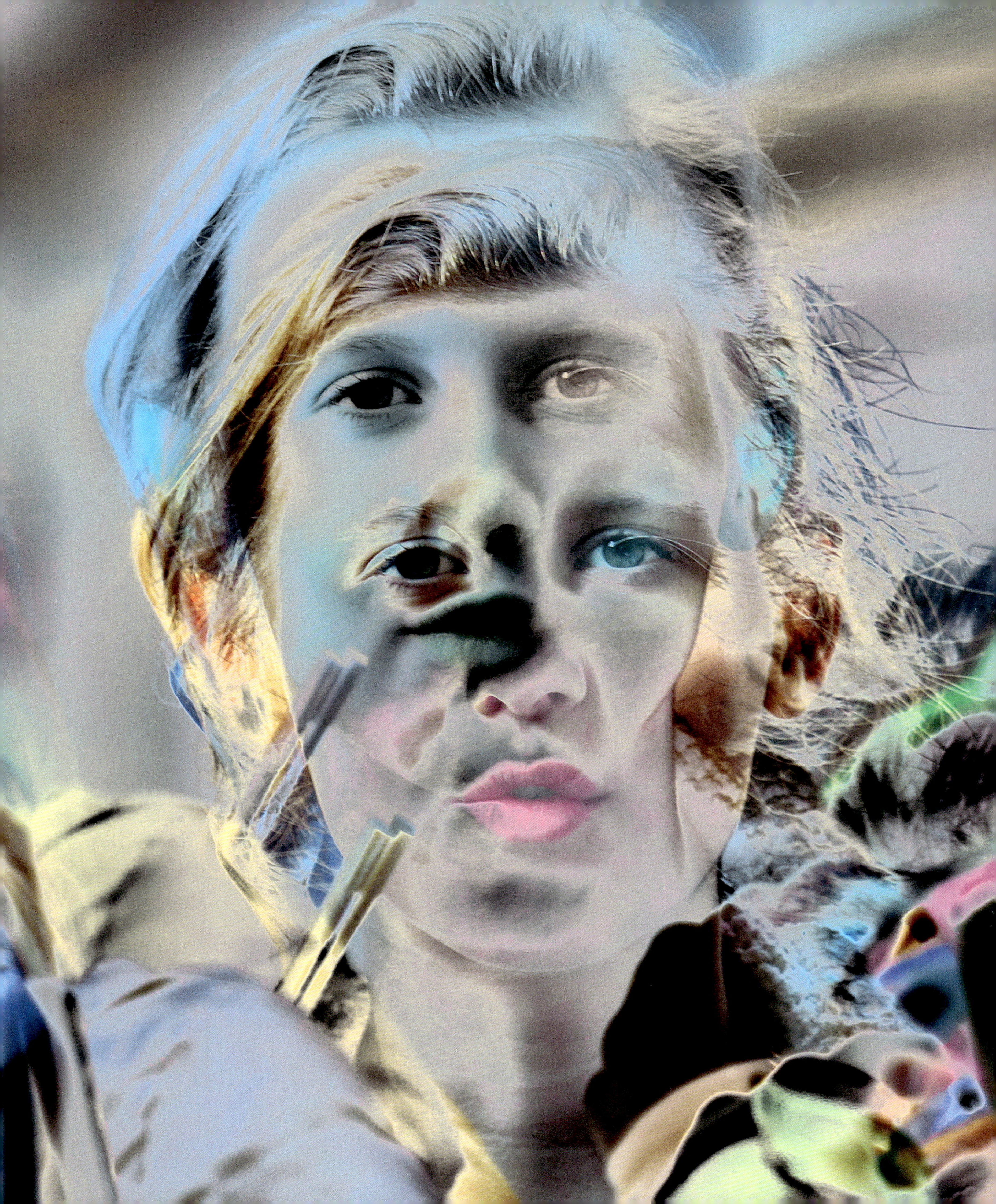

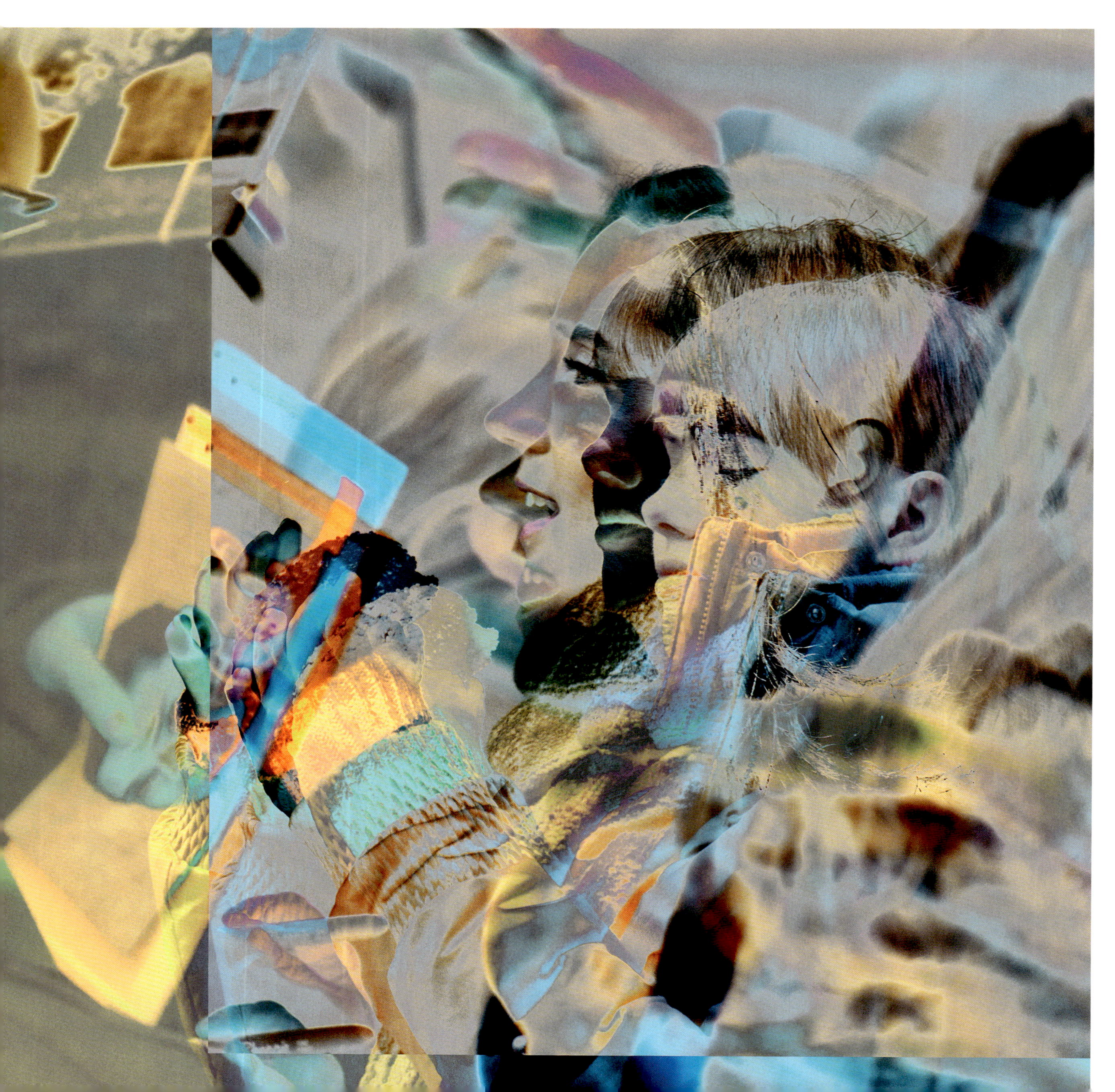

Hero Duo / Berlin / 2014

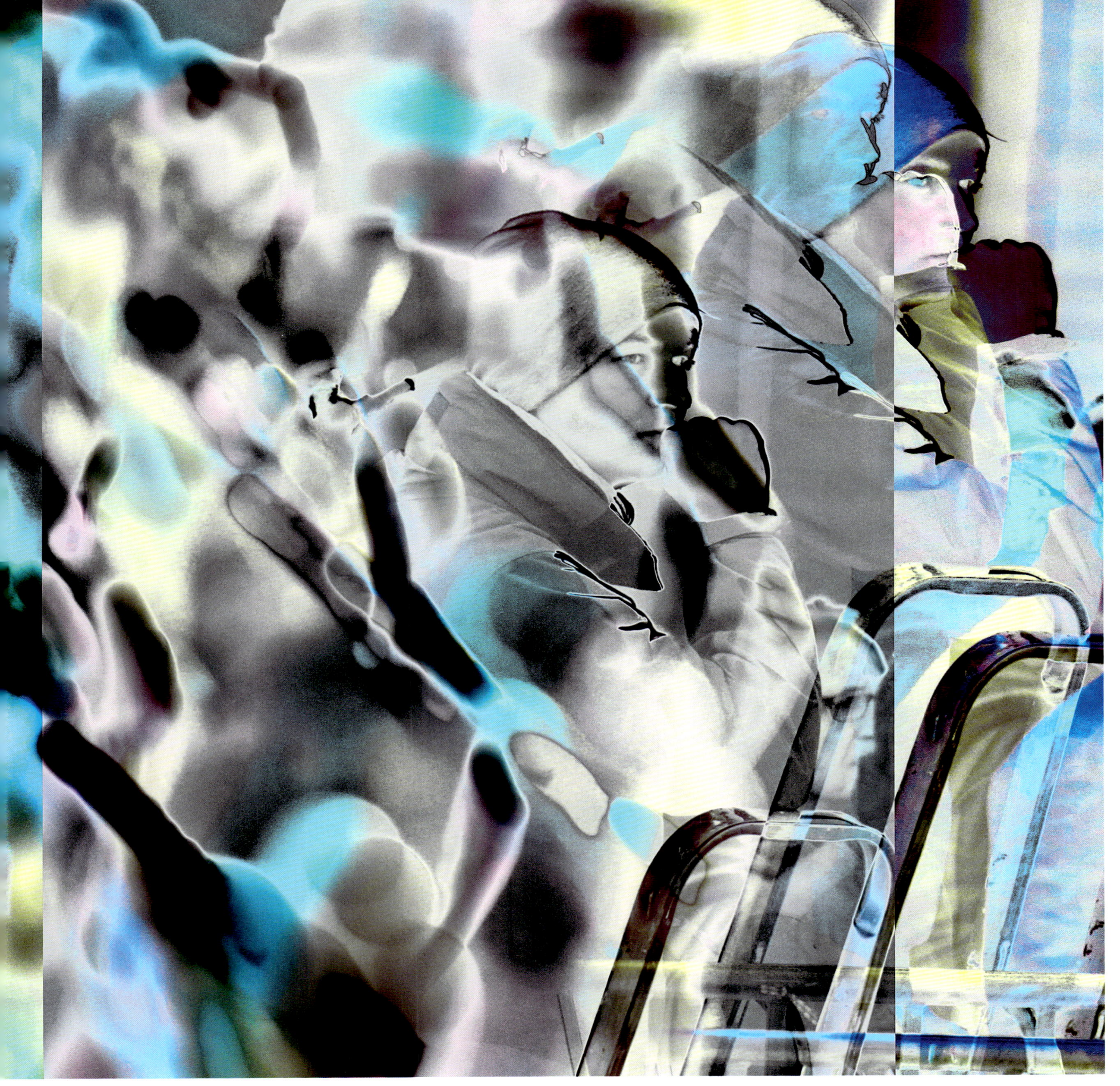

Man in the Crowd / Berlin / 2013

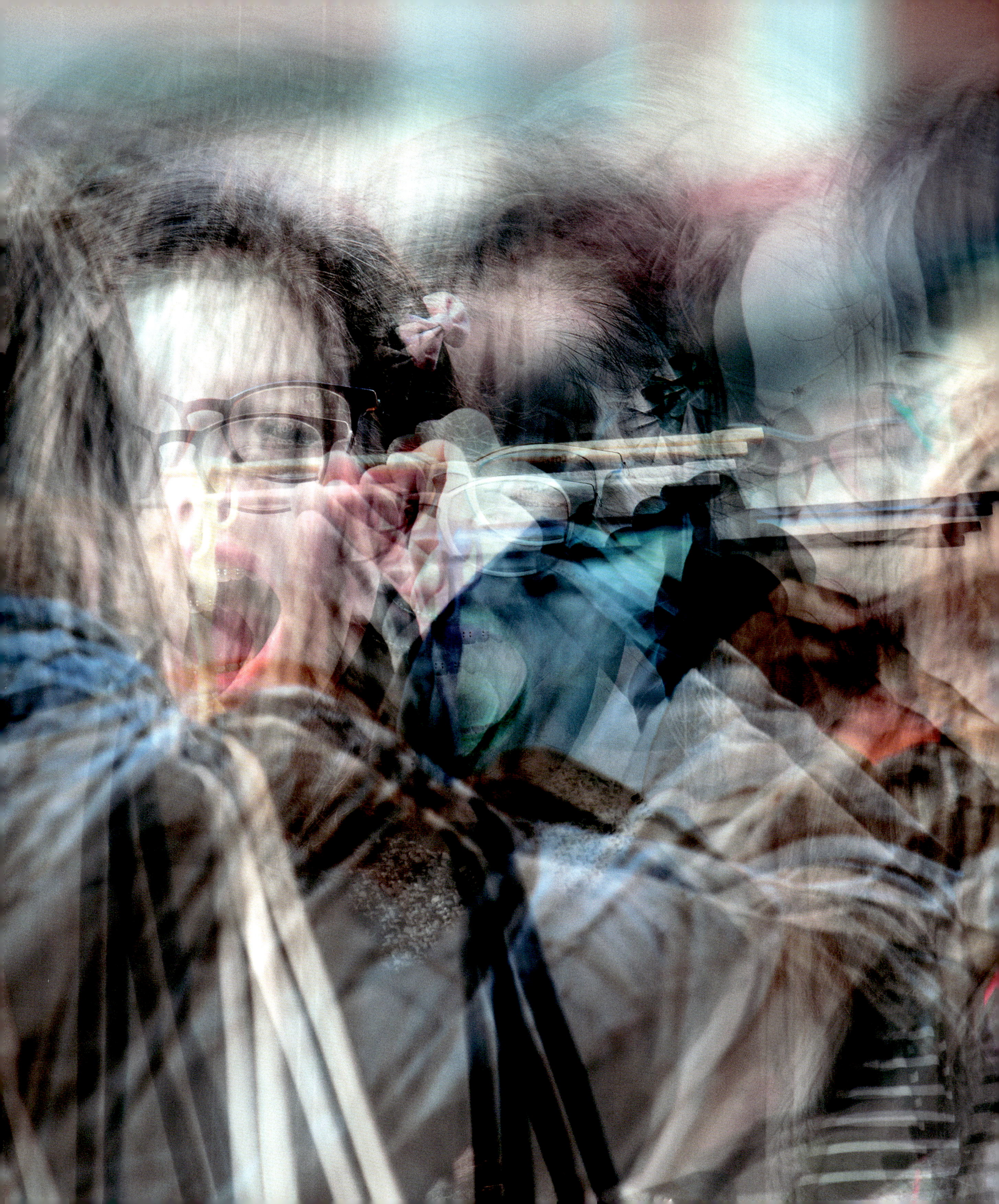

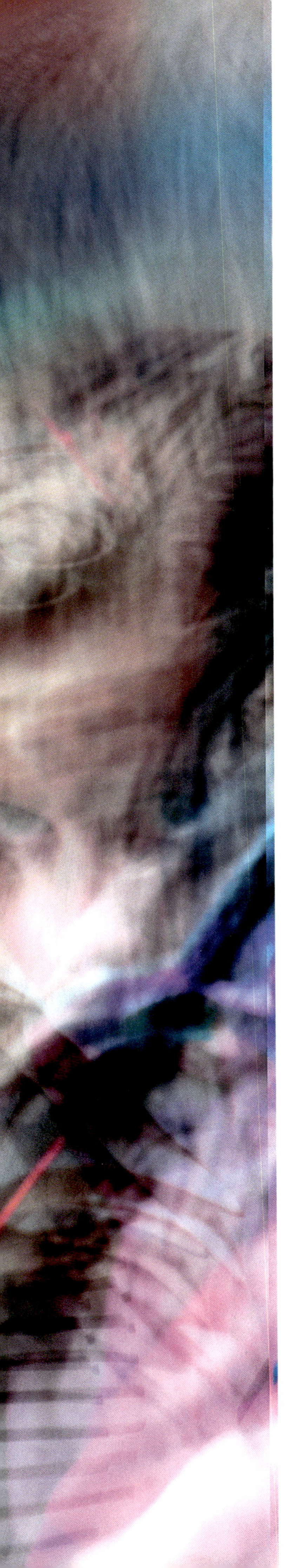

Sushi Berlin Duo / Berlin / 2014

The Army / Berlin / 2013

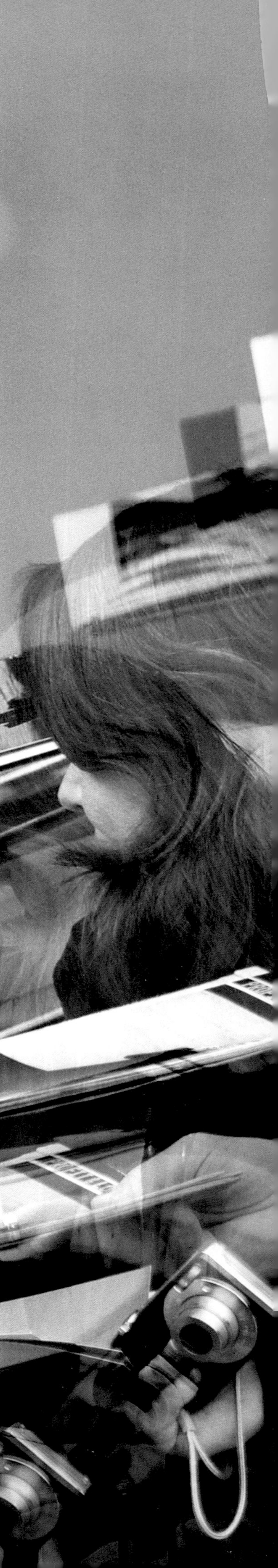

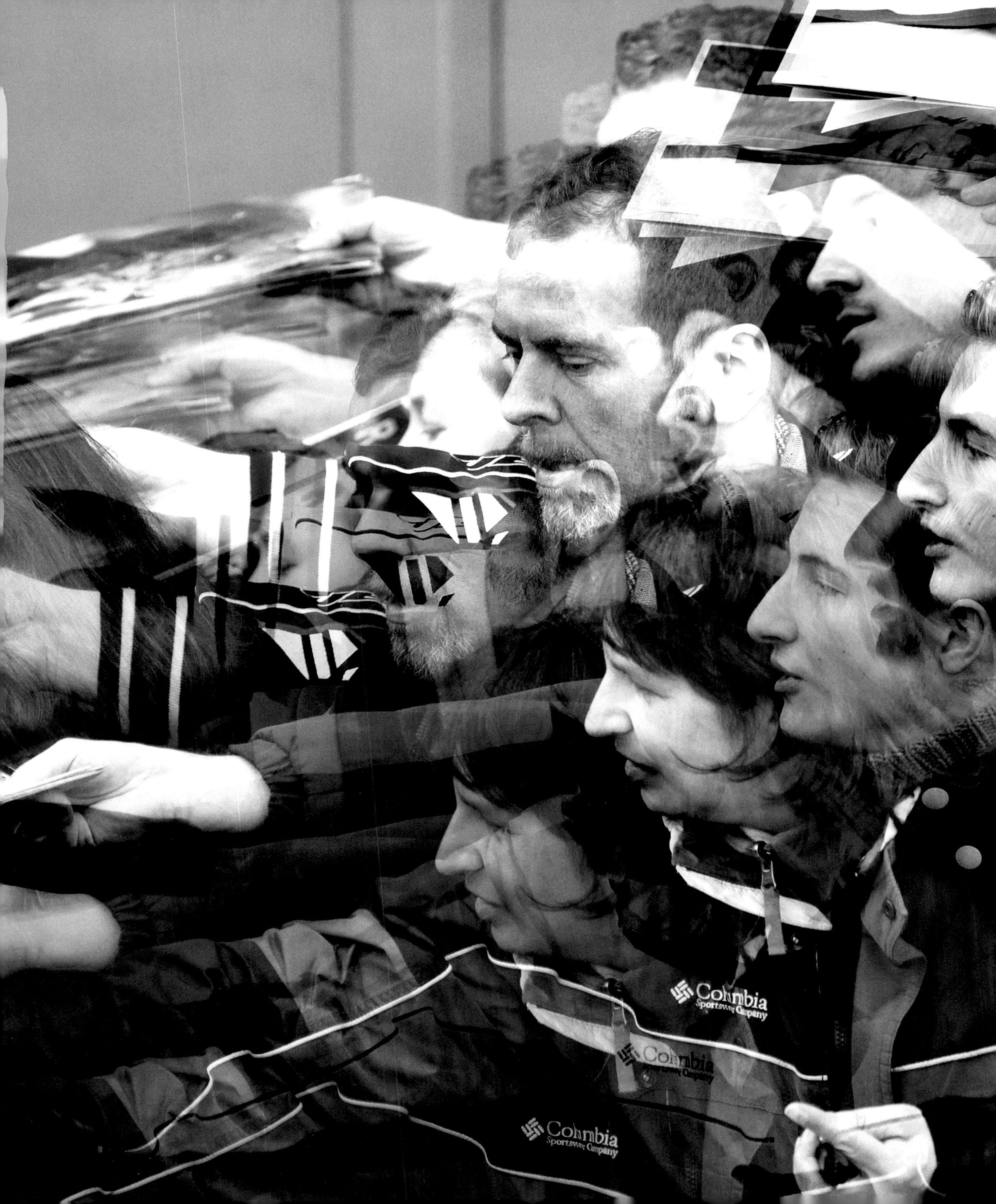

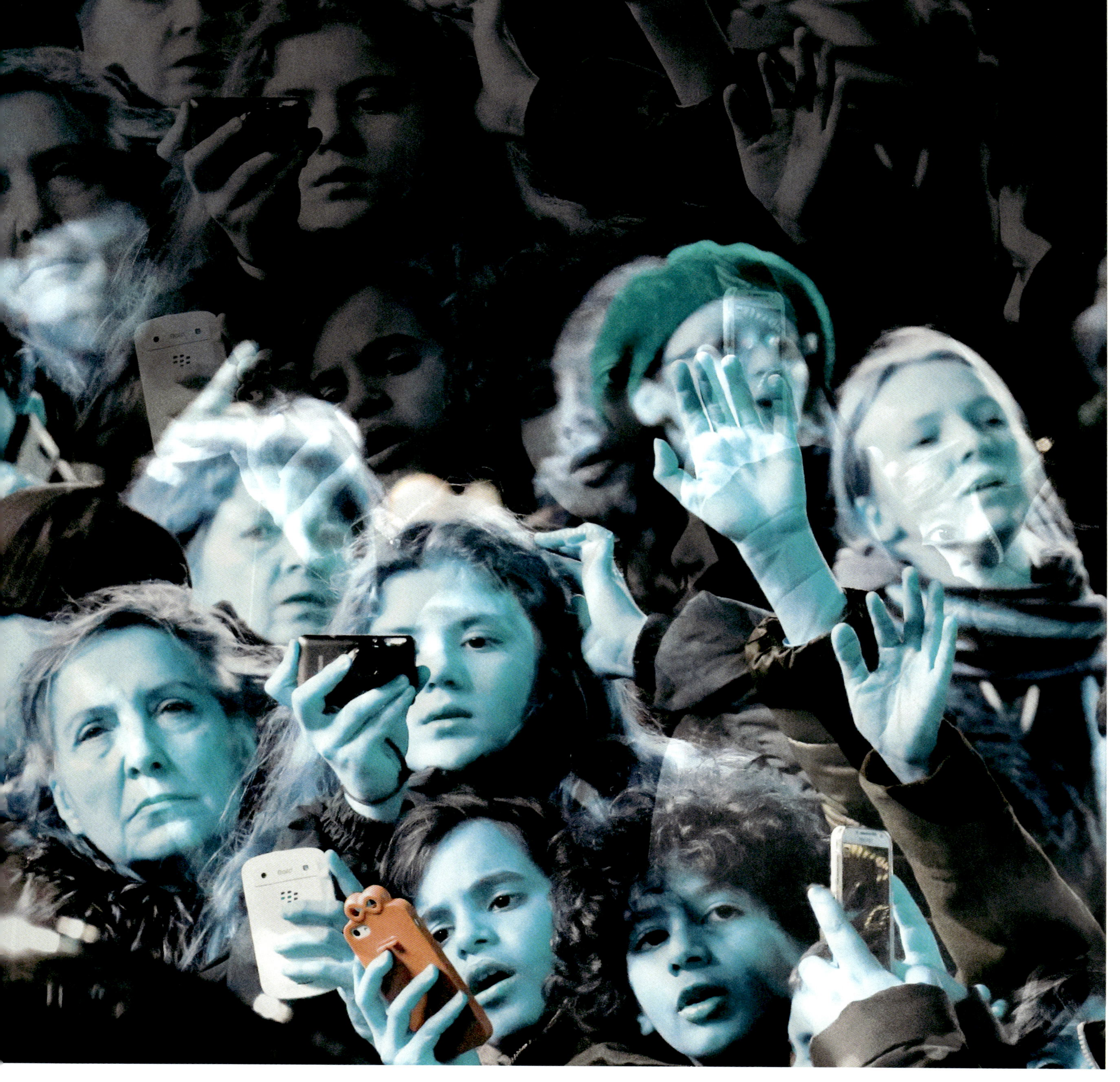

Blue Power Duo / Berlin / 2013

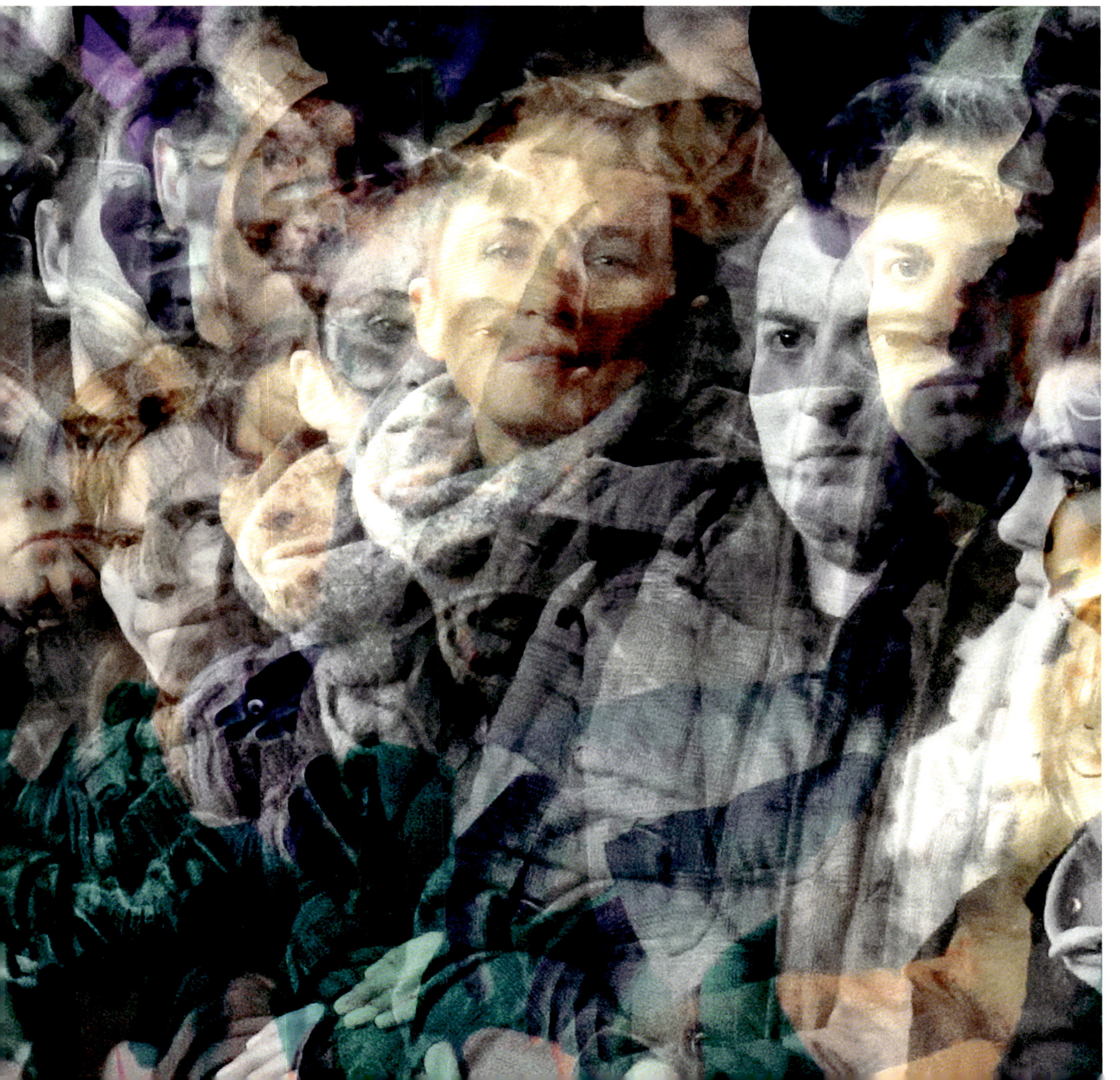

Freedom / Berlin / 2013

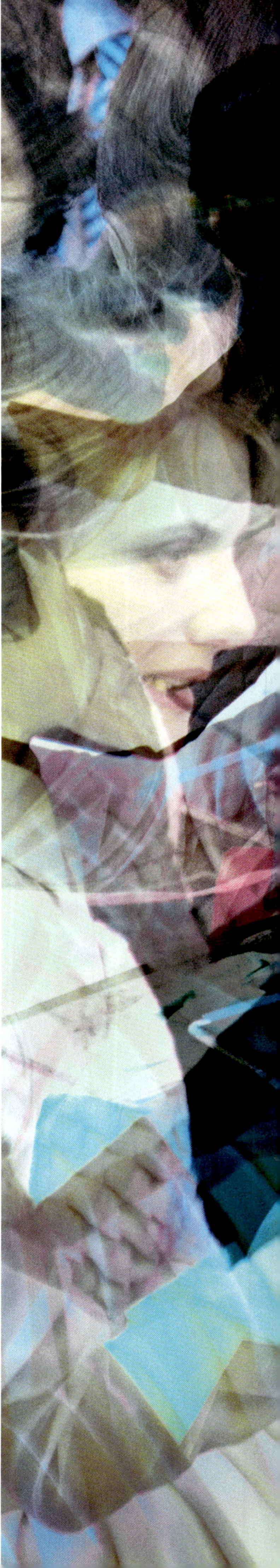

Autogramm Duo / Berlin / 2014

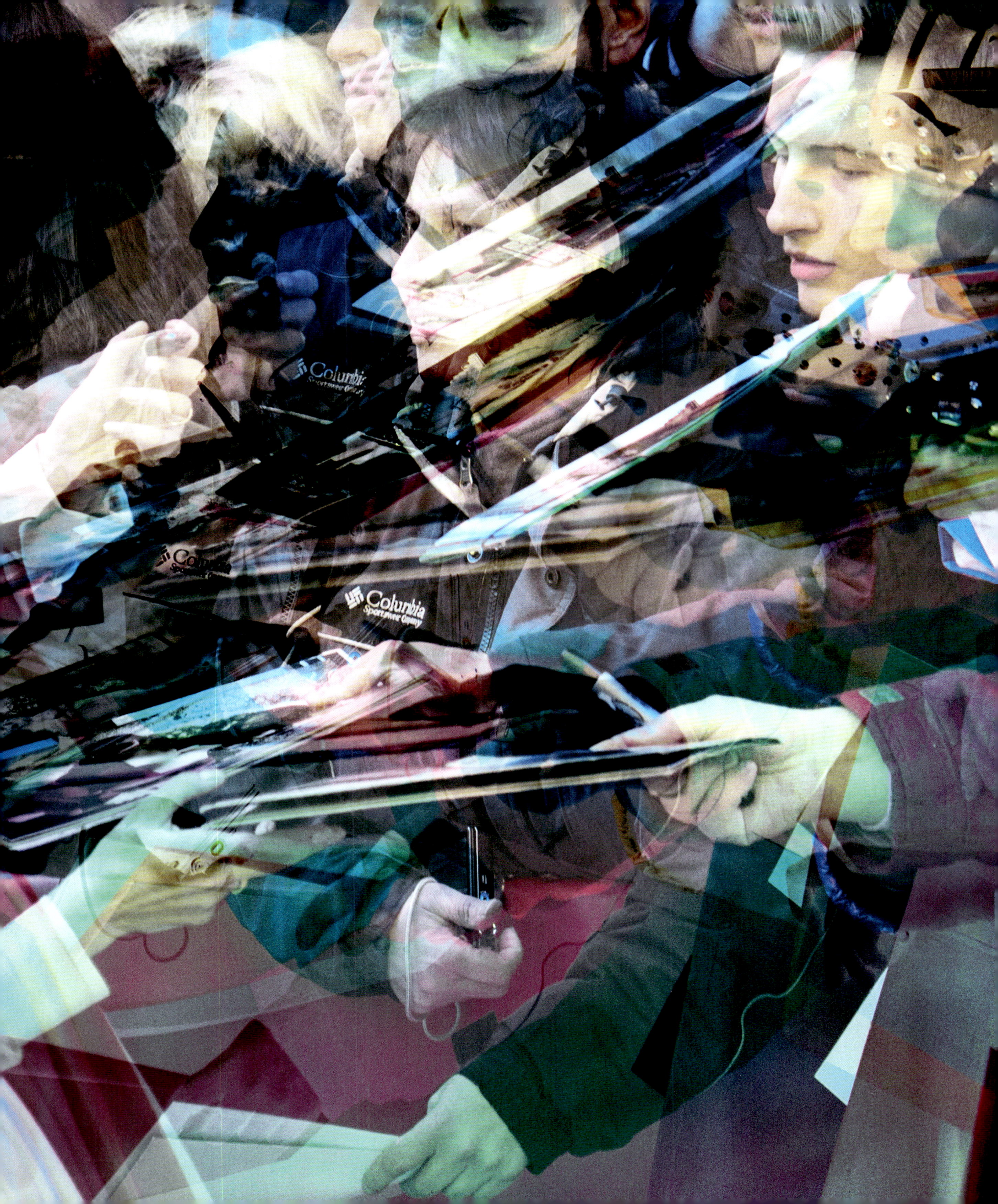

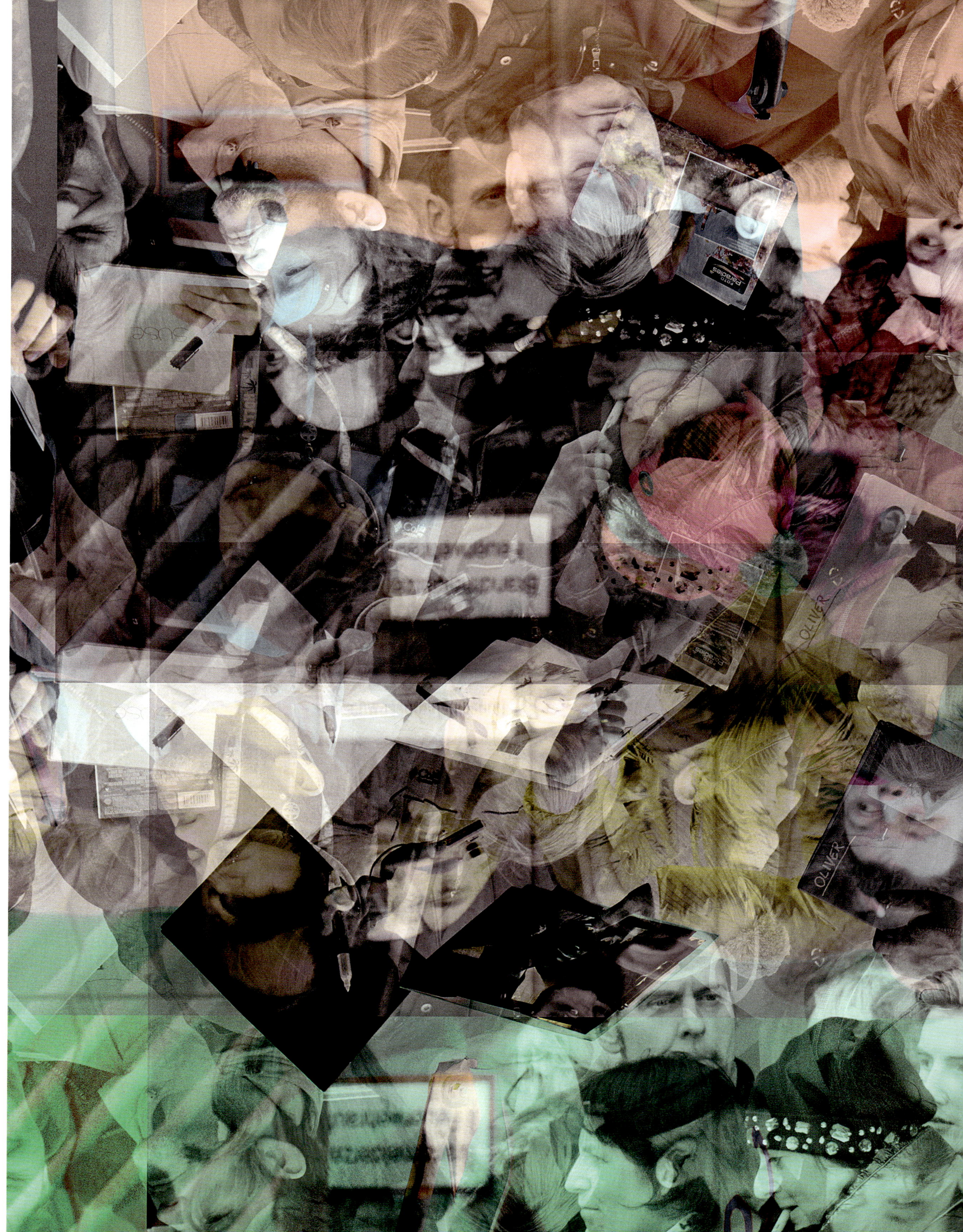

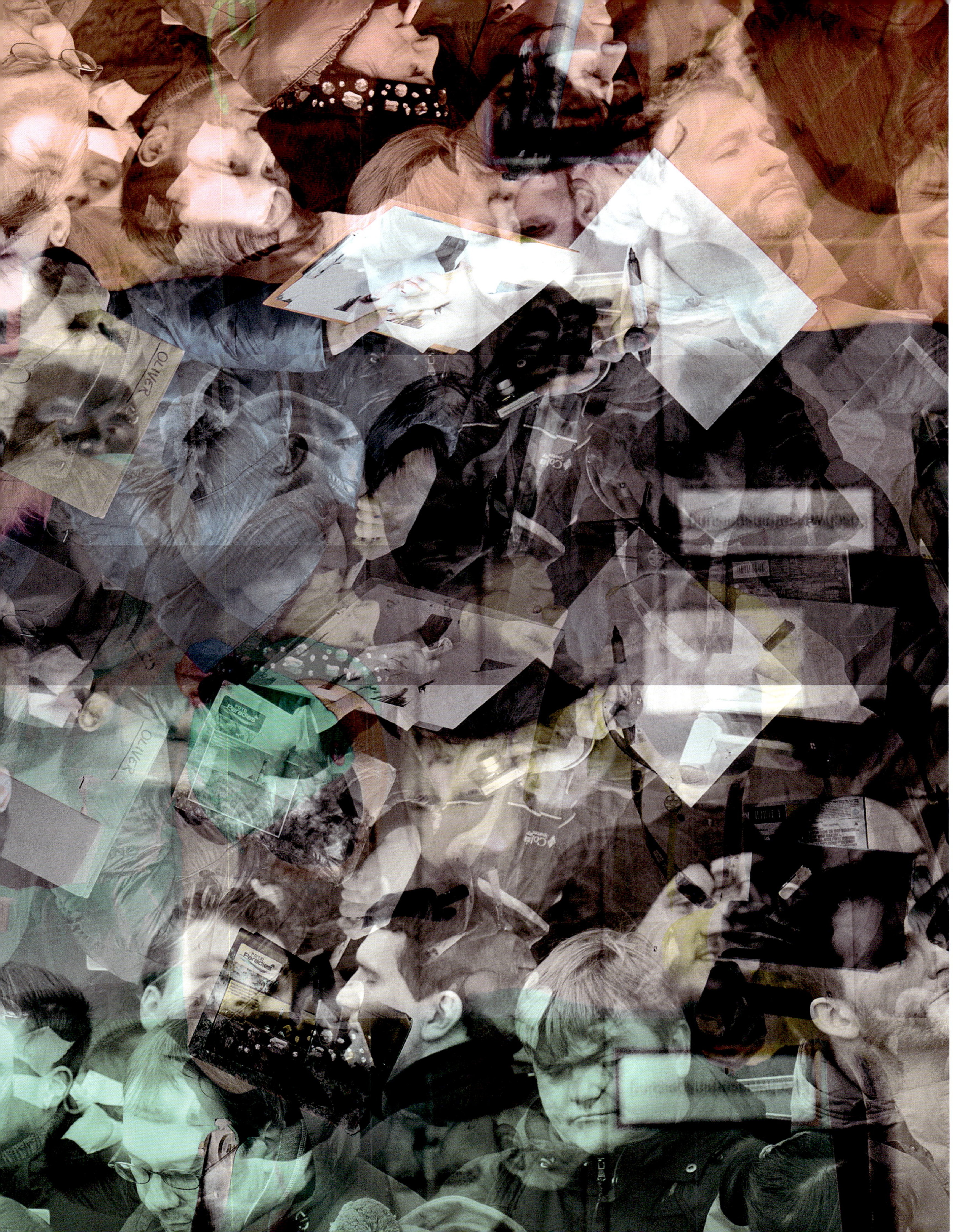

Lonely People Duo / Berlin / 2013

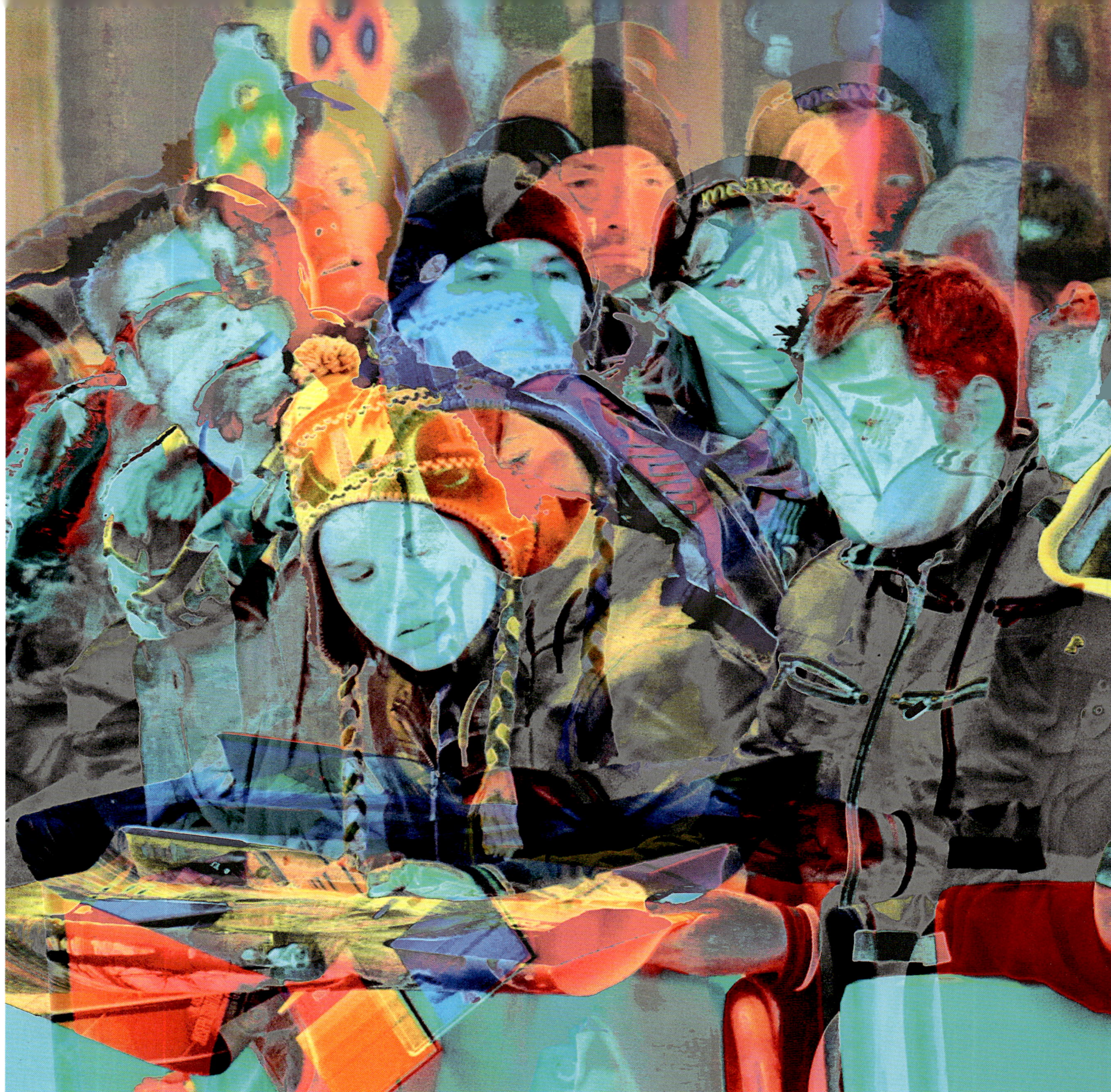

Red and Blue Army / Berlin / 2013

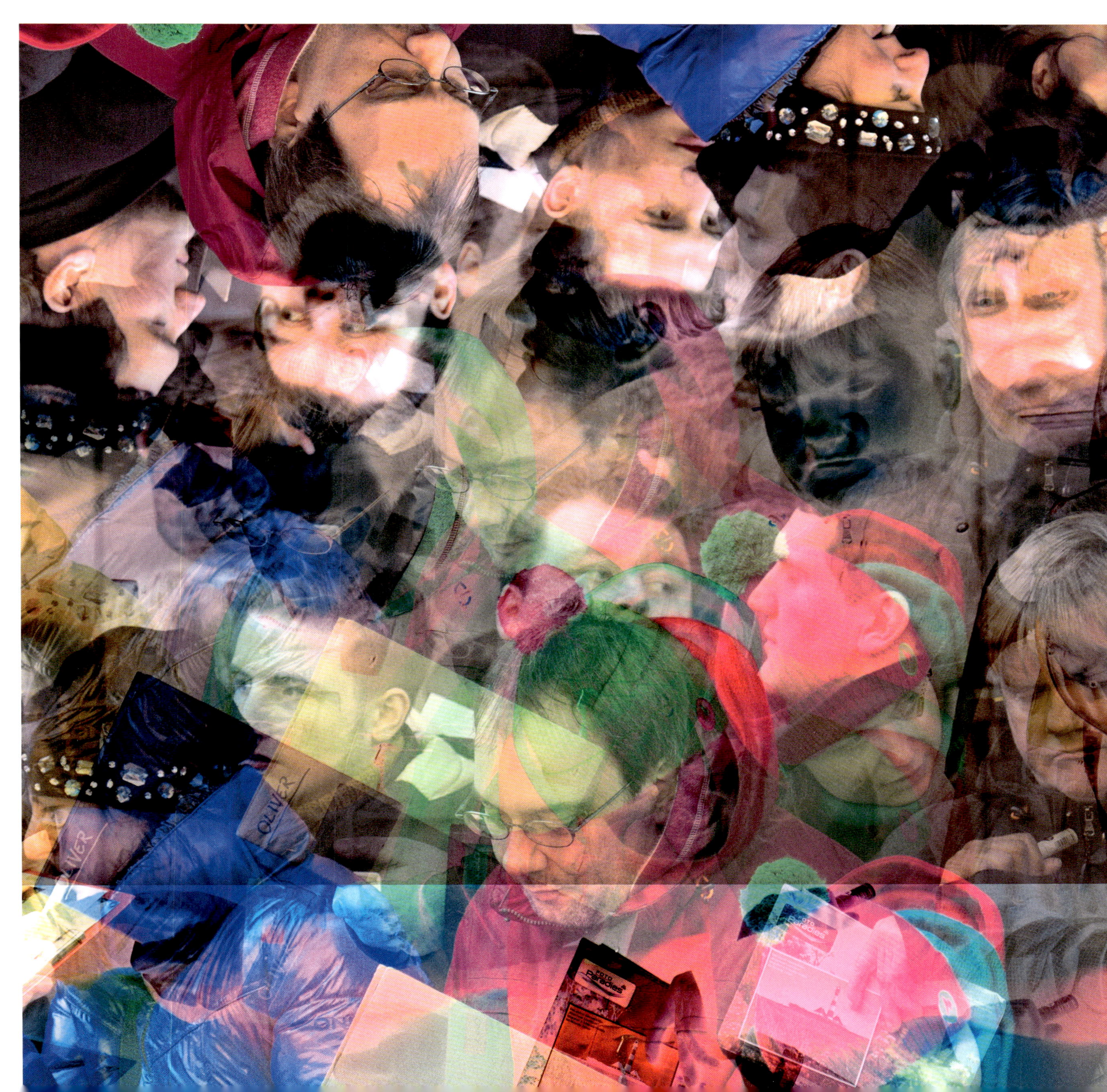

Mix of Heads Duo / Berlin / 2014

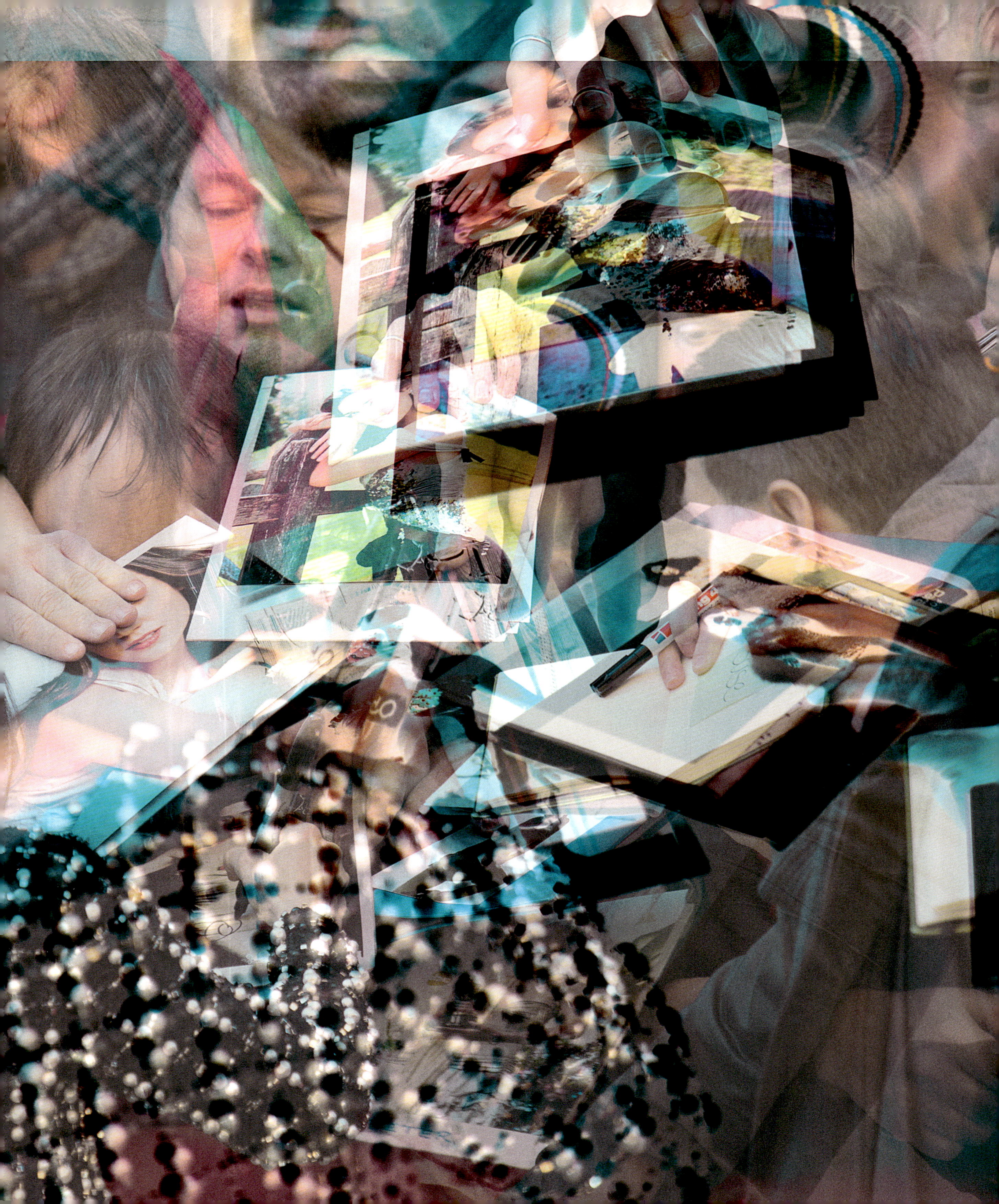

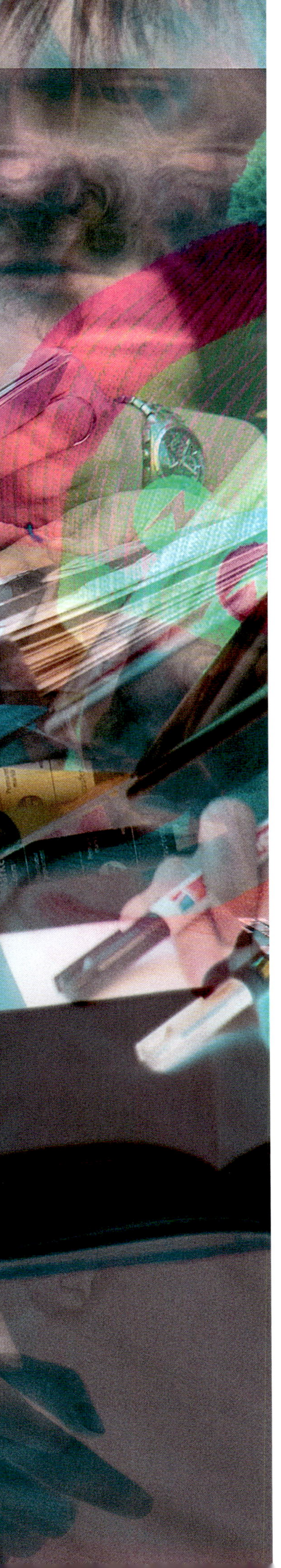

The Idol Duo / Berlin / 2014

Legs and Legs Duo / Berlin / 2014

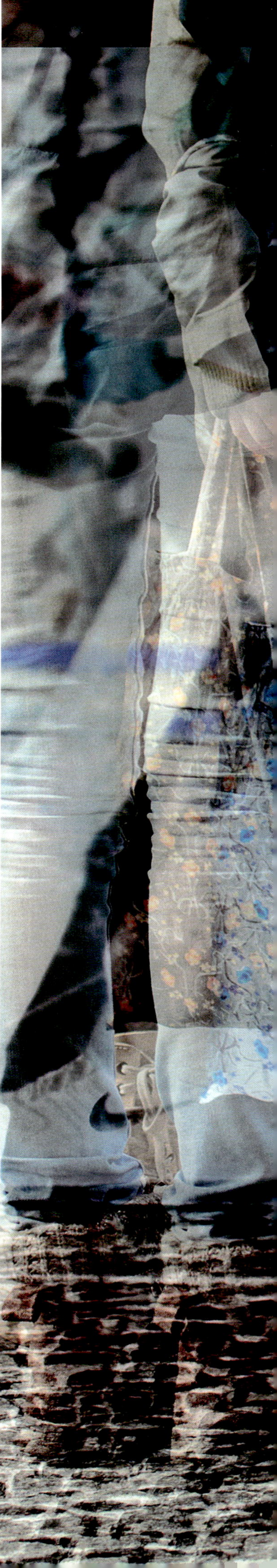

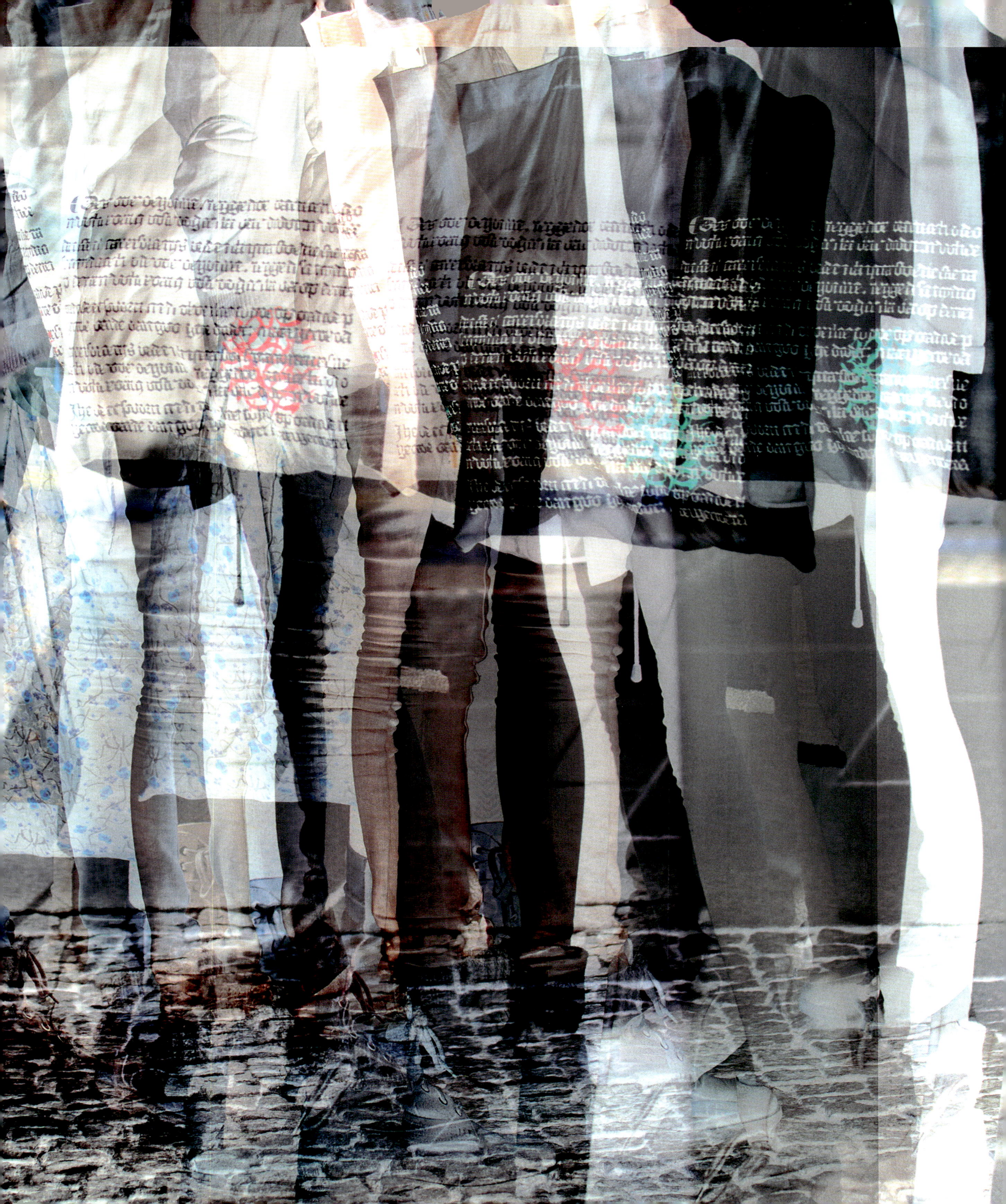

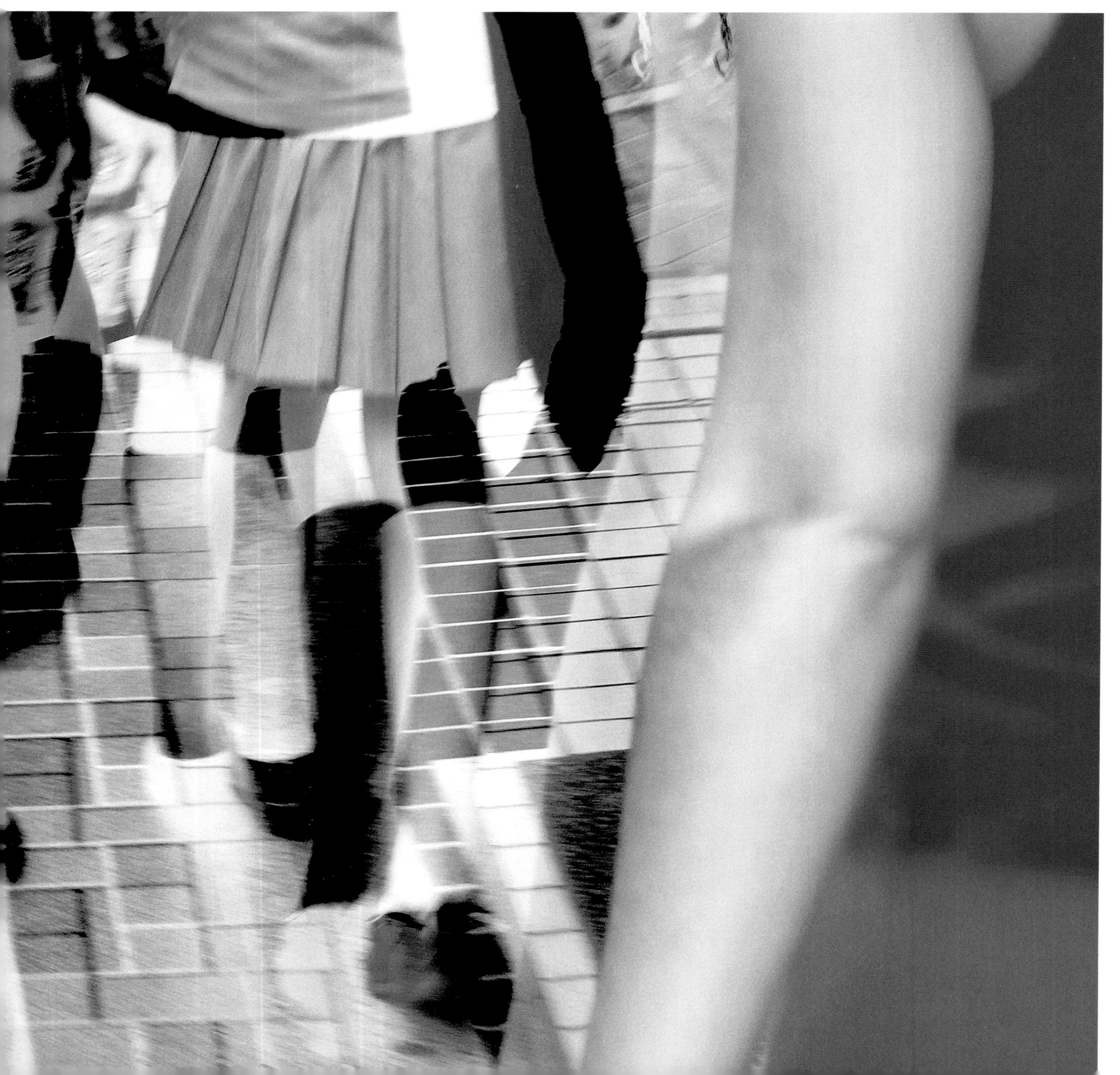

Tokyo Girls Grey Duo / Tokyo / 2008

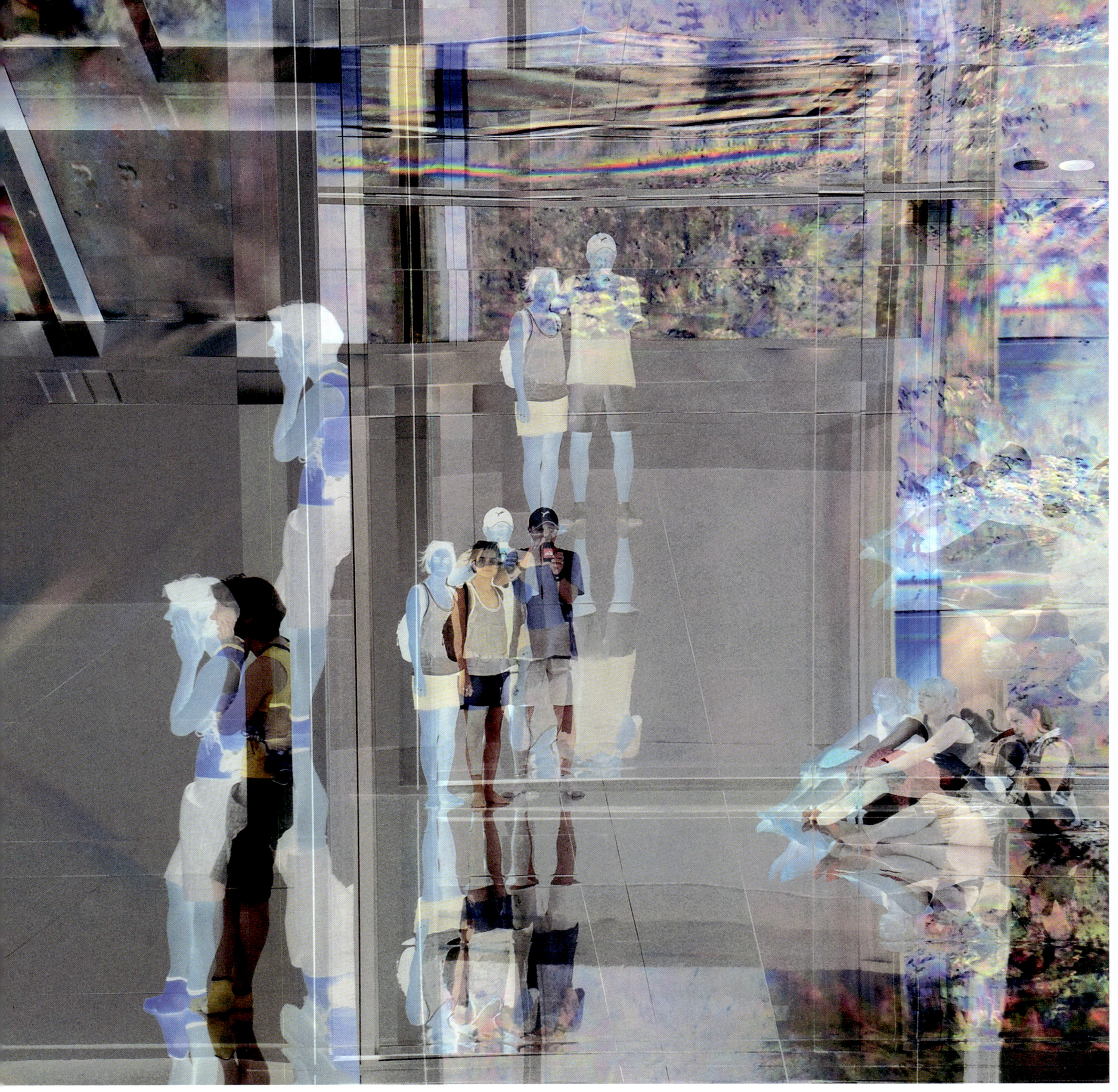

Family Tour Duo / Venice / 2013

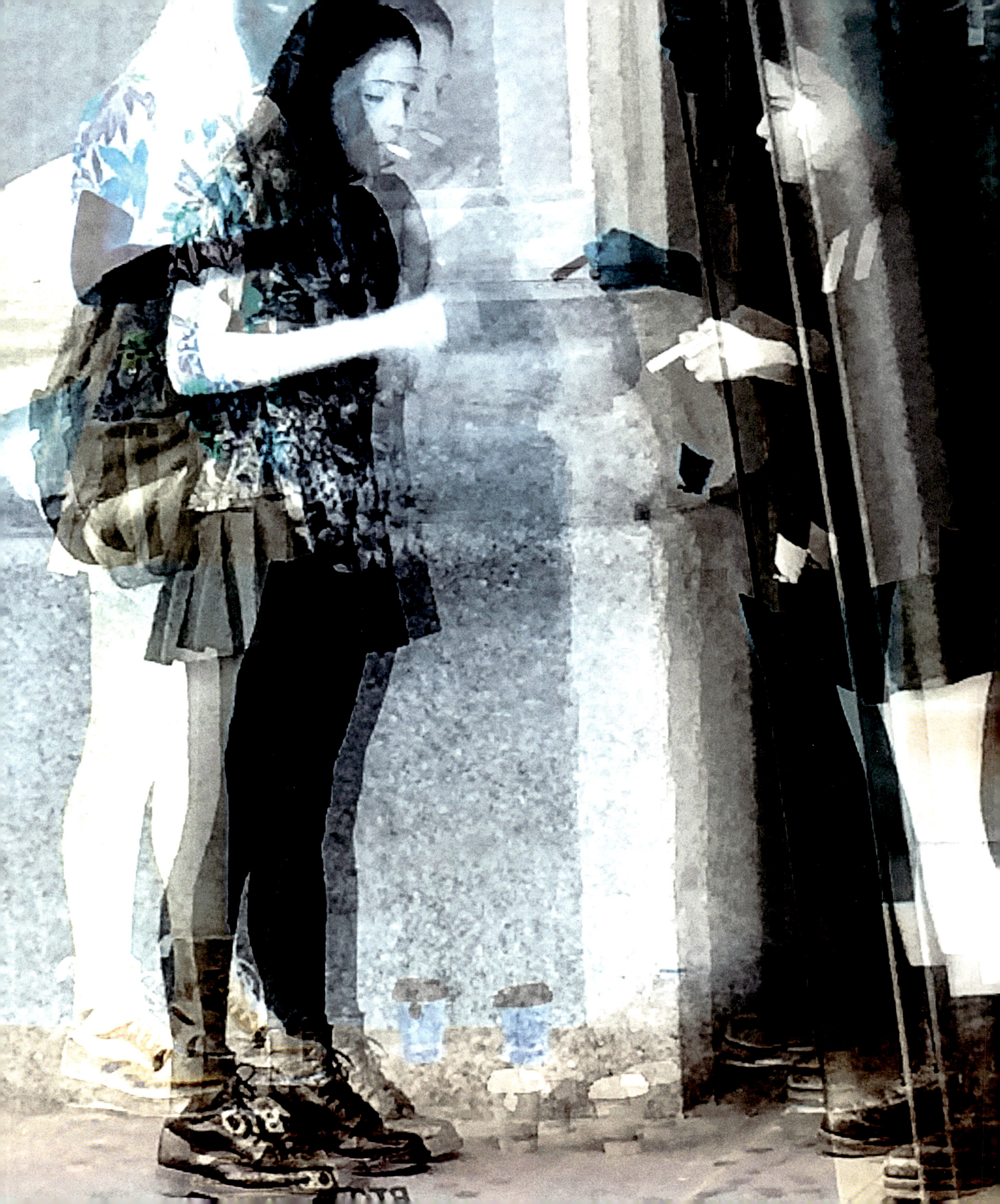

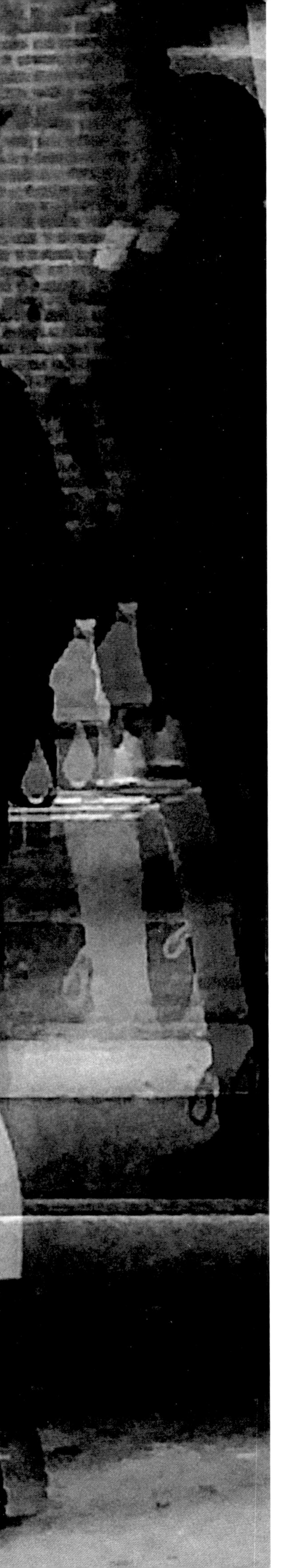

Paris Taxi Duo / Paris / 2013

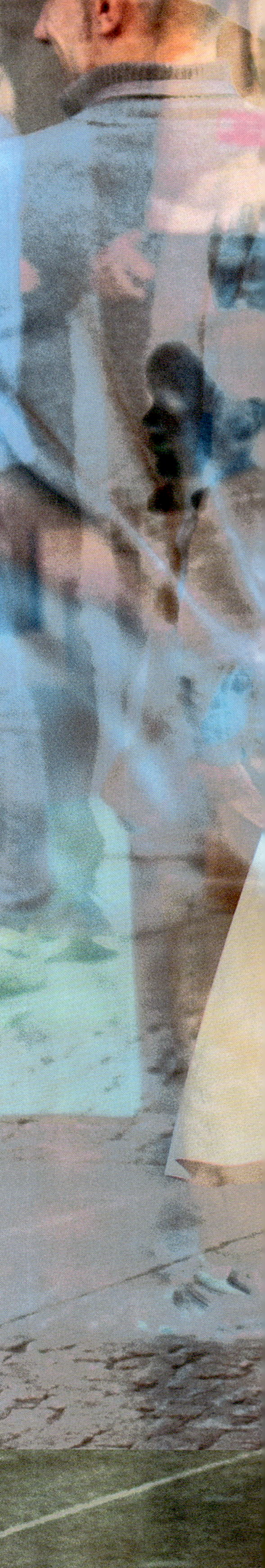

Berlinale Duo / Berlin / 2014

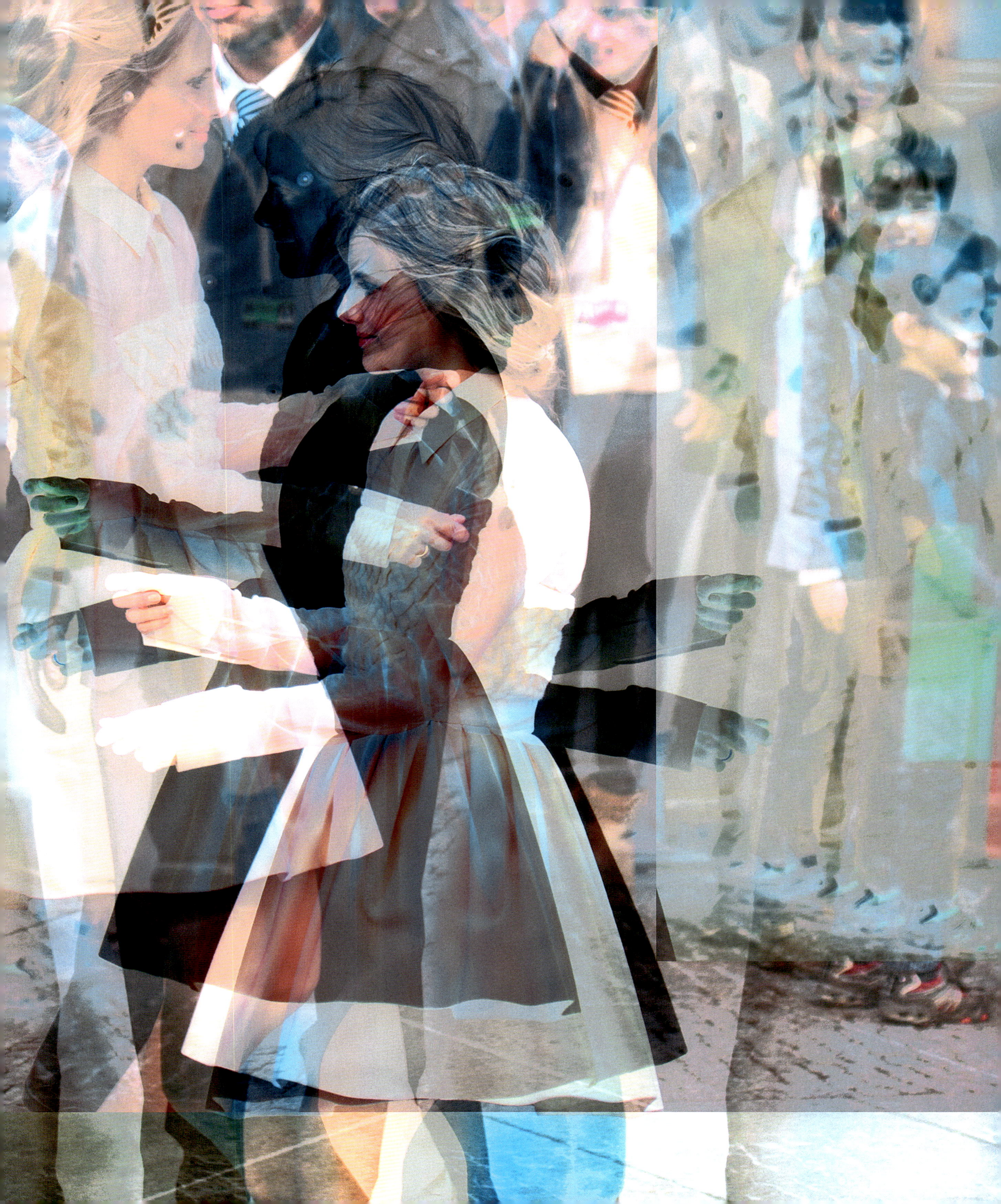

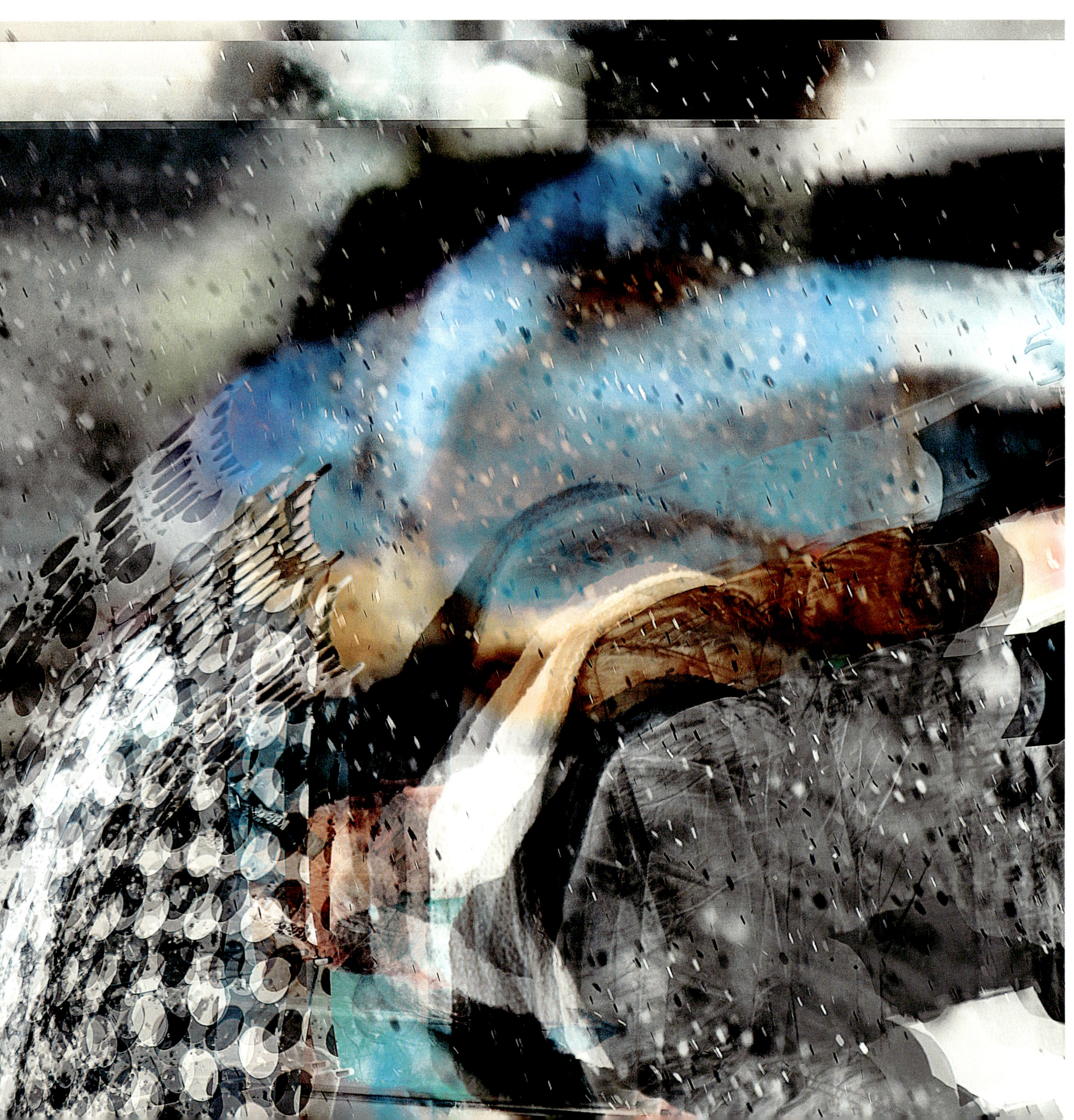

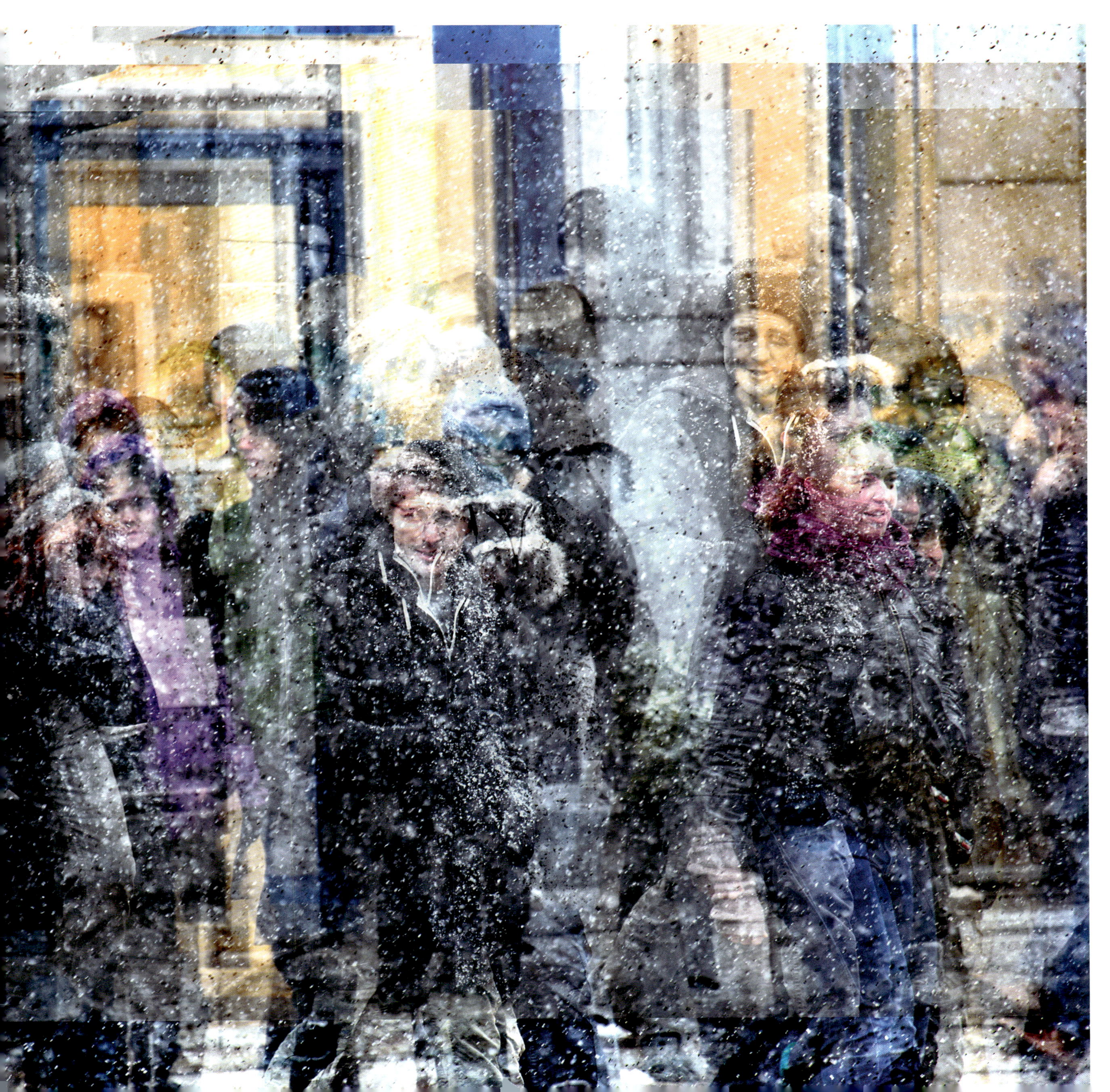

Snow People / Berlin / 2014

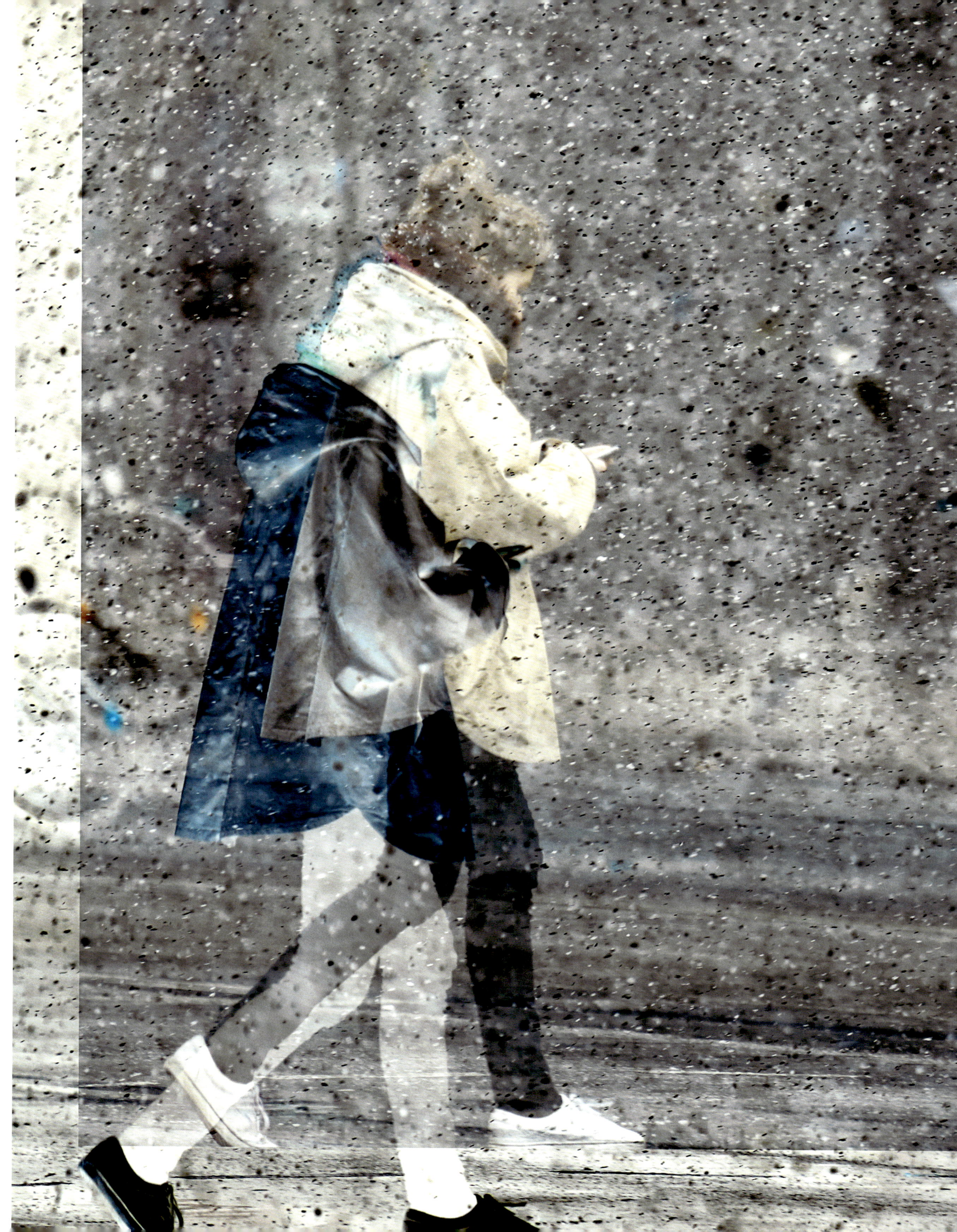

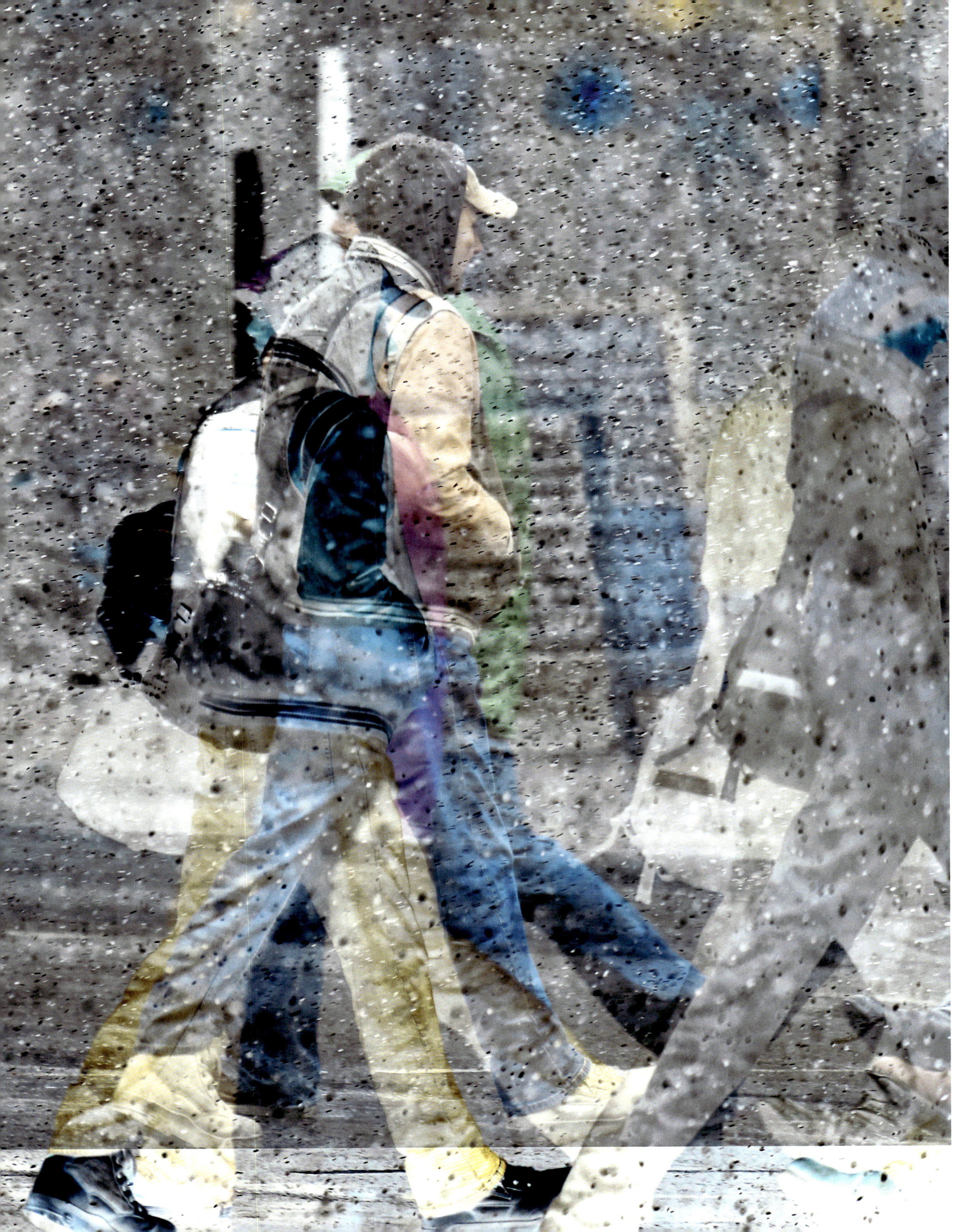

Walking Duo / Berlin / 2013

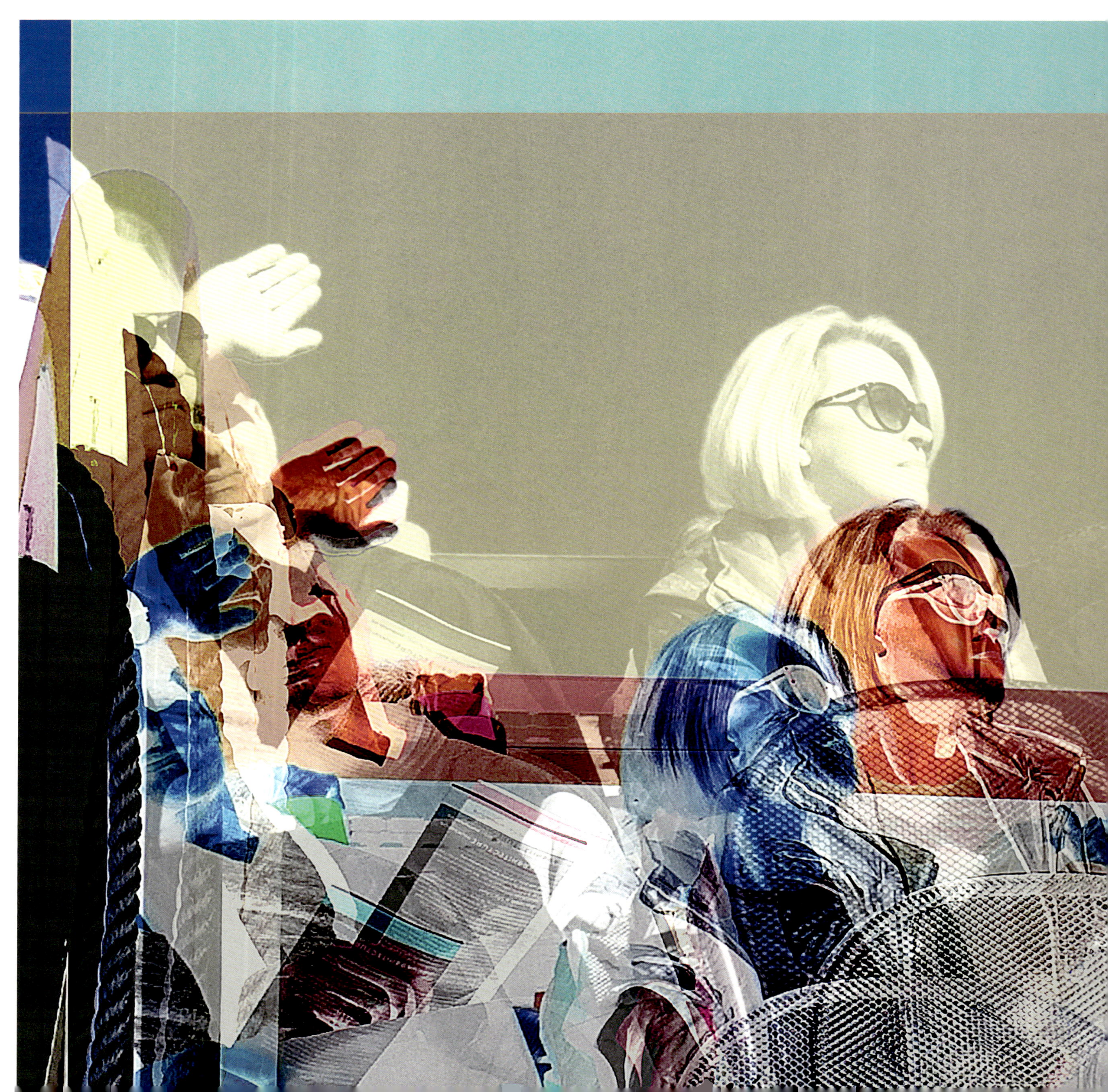

Chicago Duo / Chicago / 2014

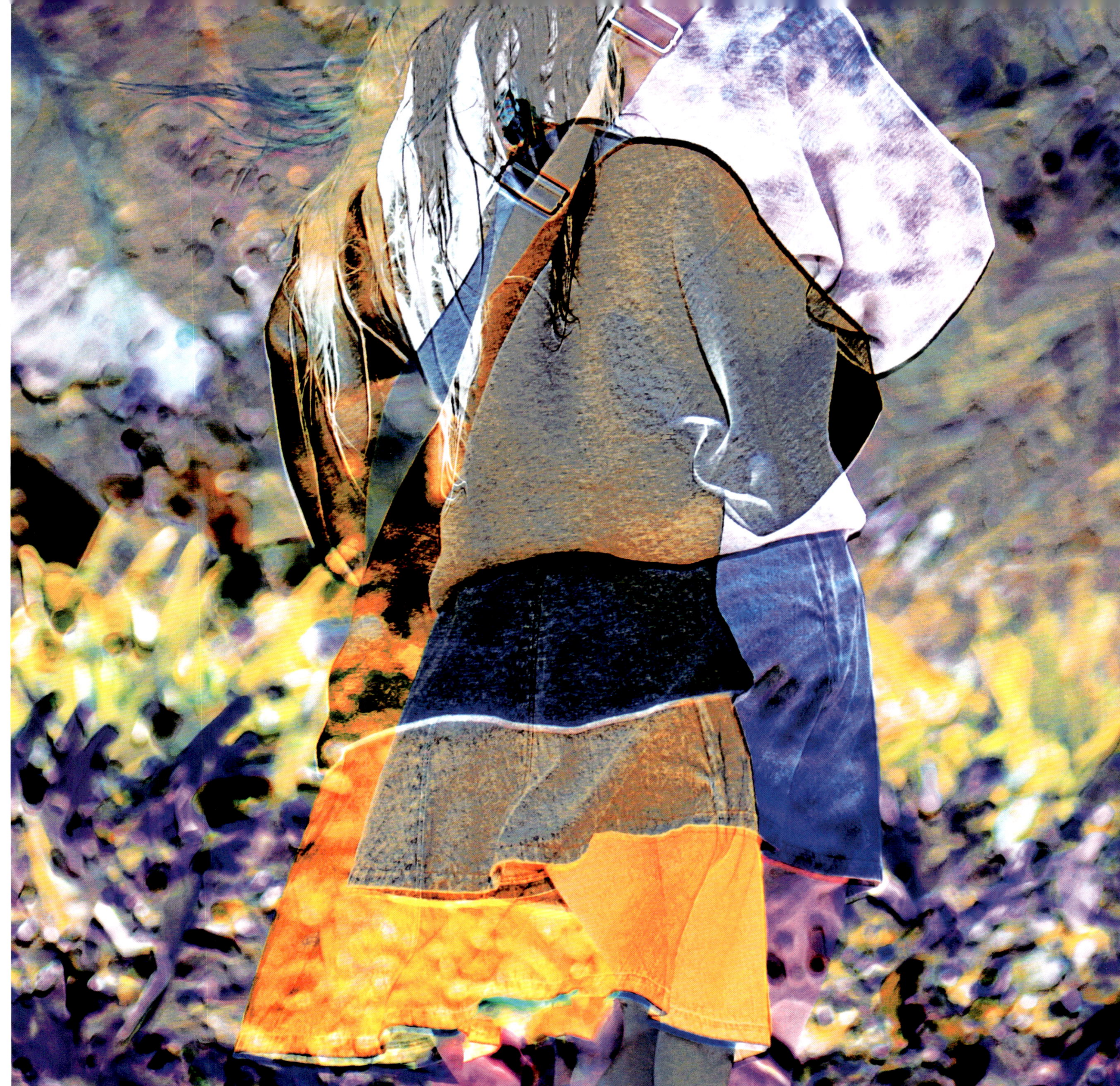

Hawaiian Girl Duo / Hawaii / 2013

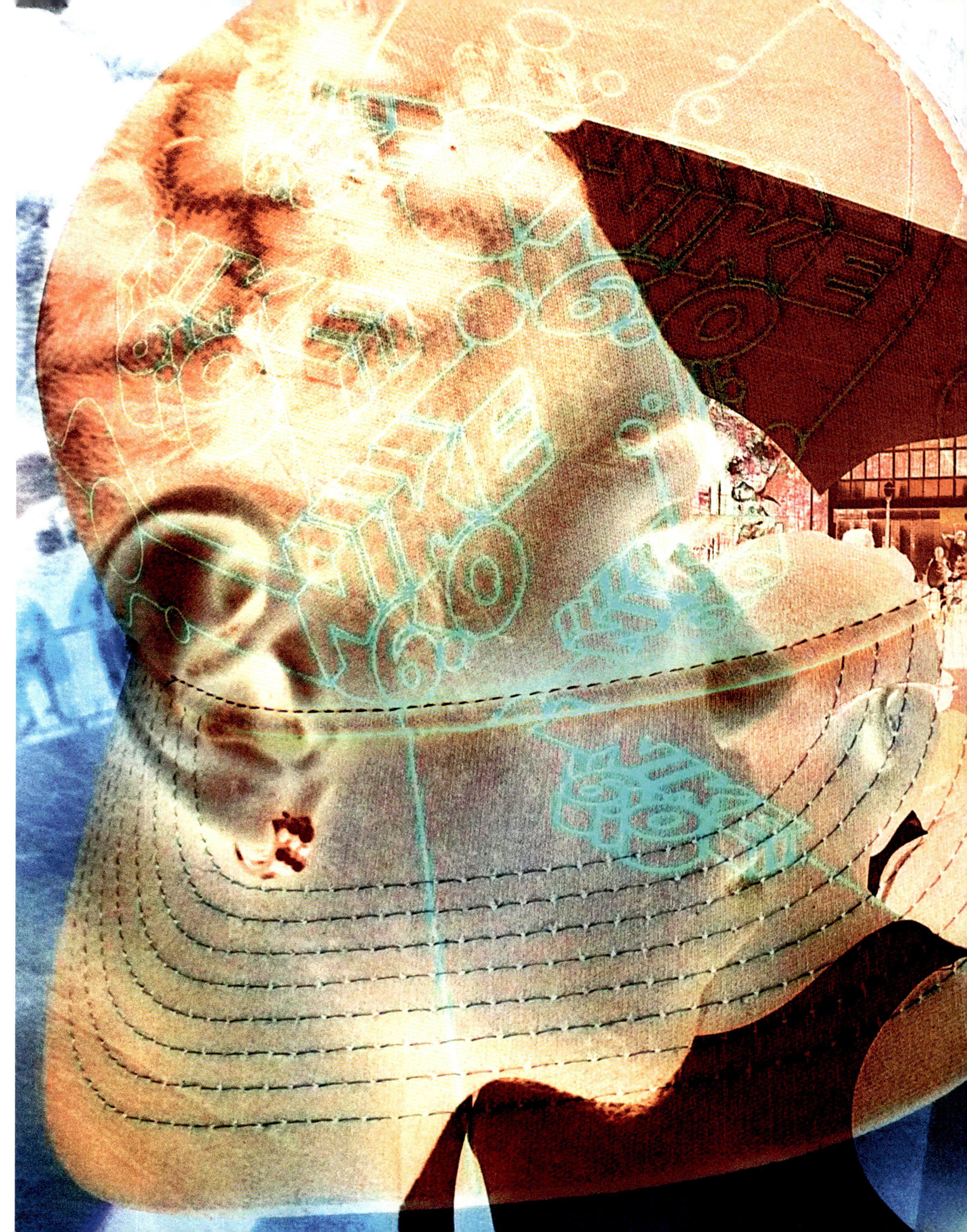

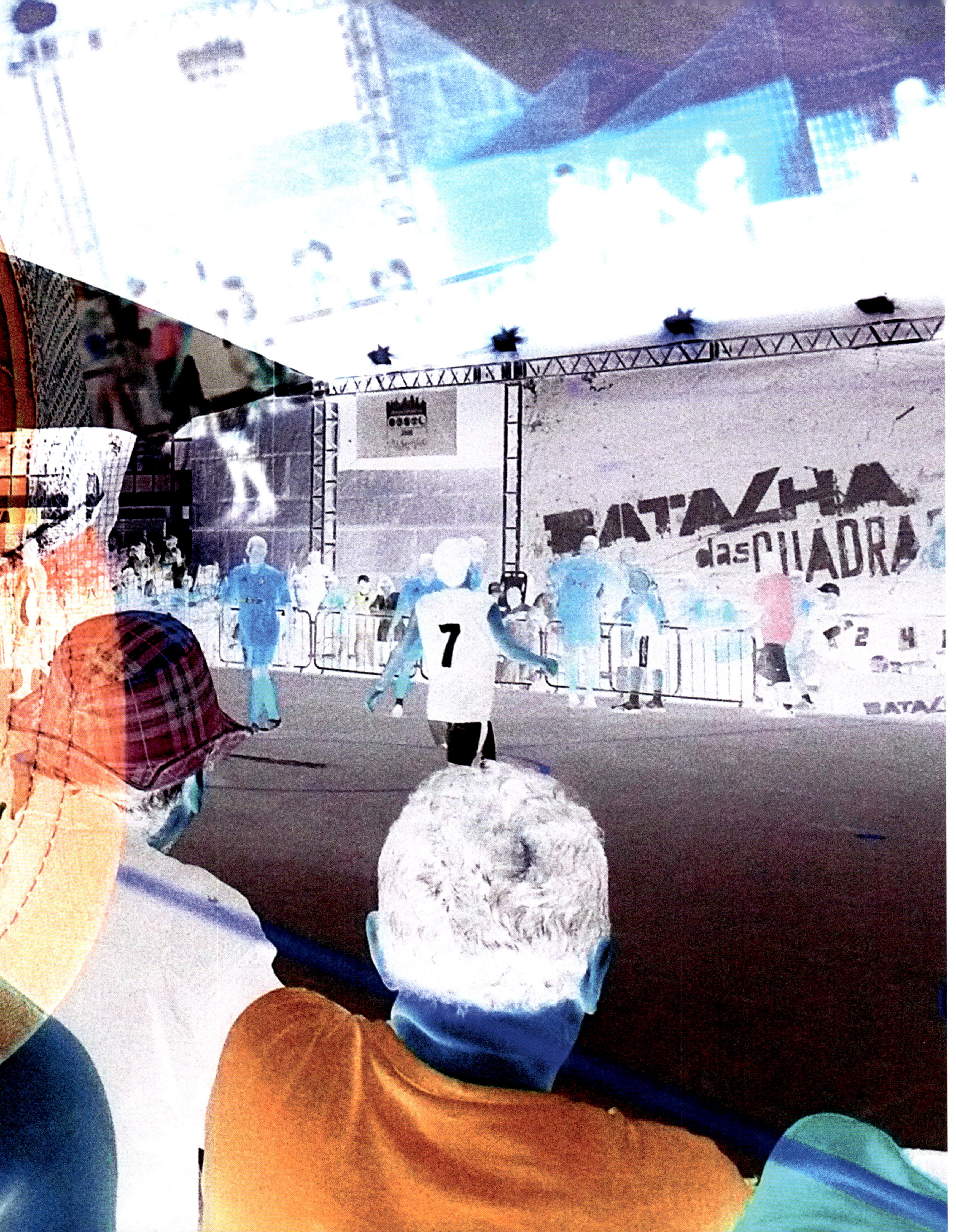

Anhangabaú Duo / São Paulo / 2010

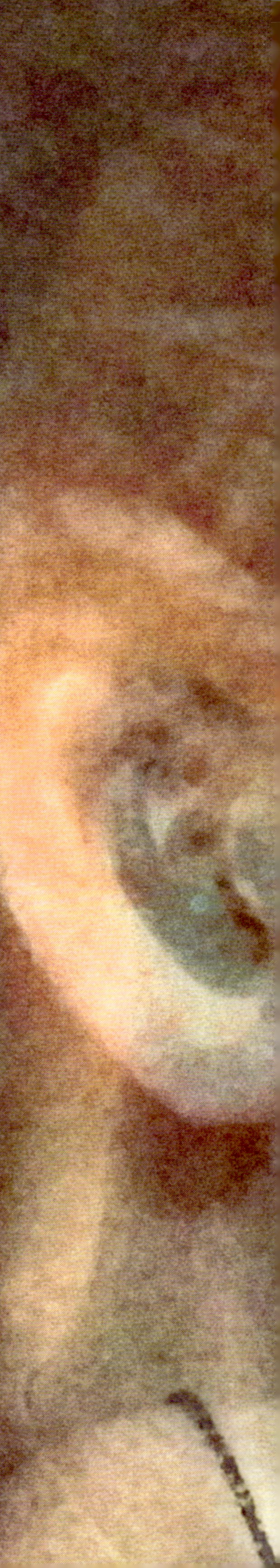

Luiza Duo / São Paulo / 2015

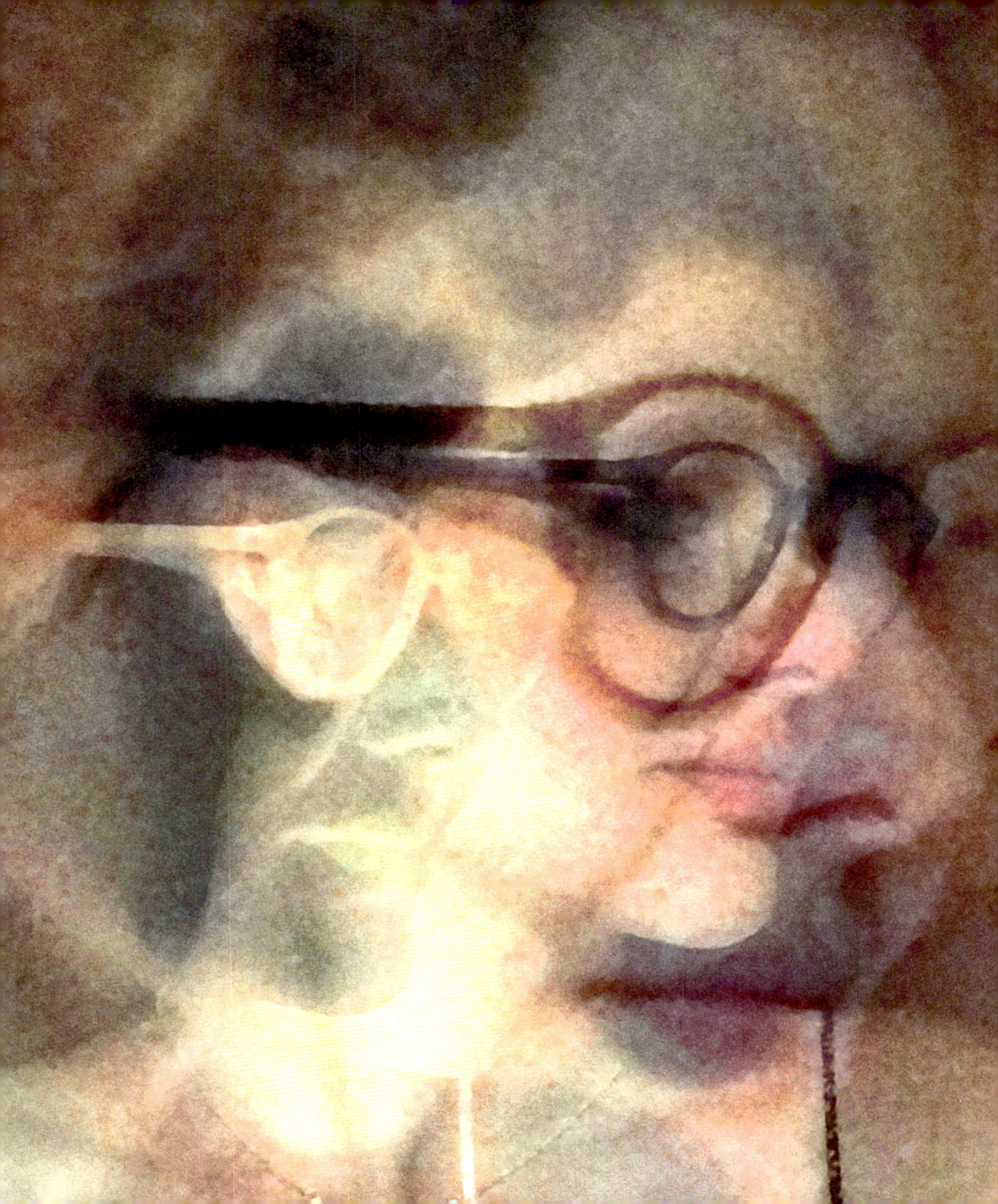

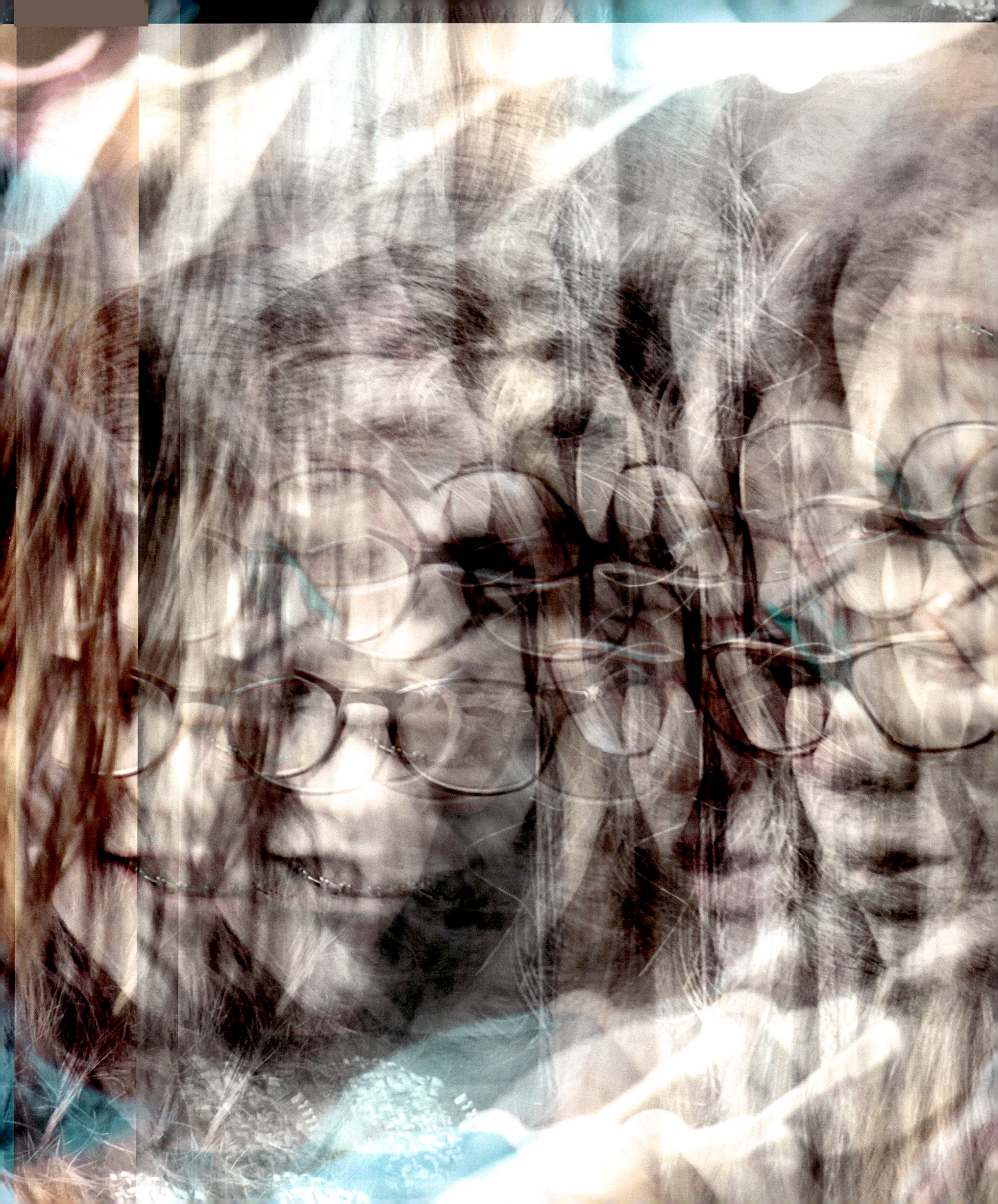

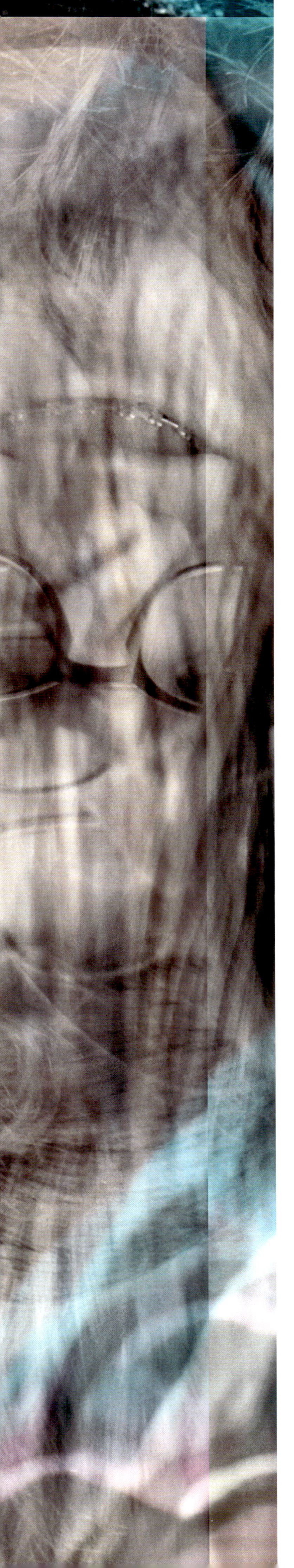

Girls Duo Triple / Berlin / 2014

Queen Duo / São Paulo / 2013

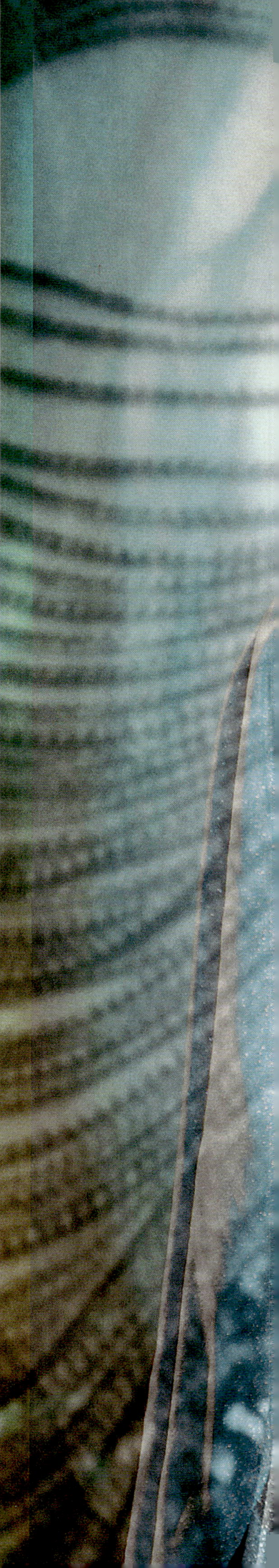

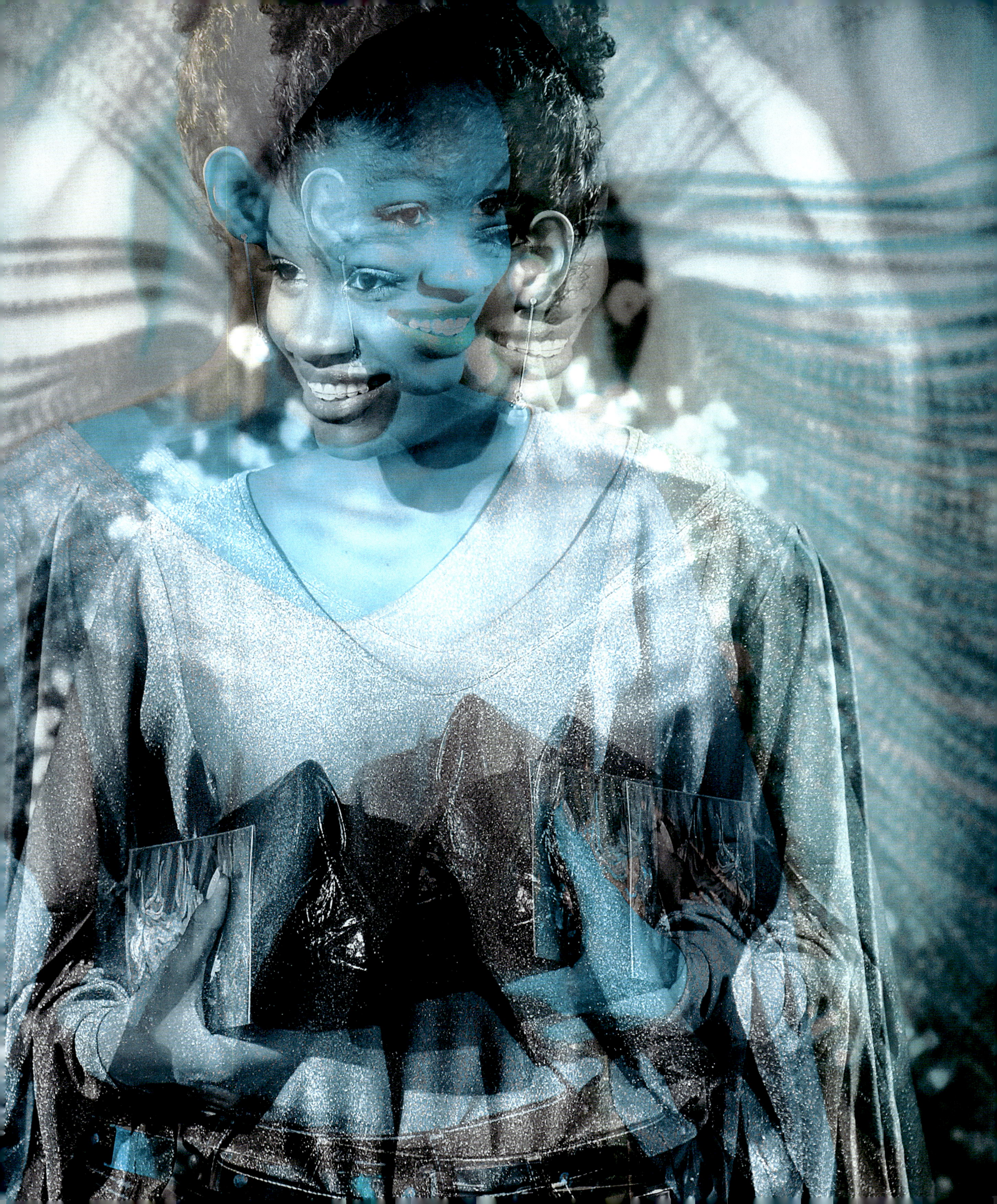

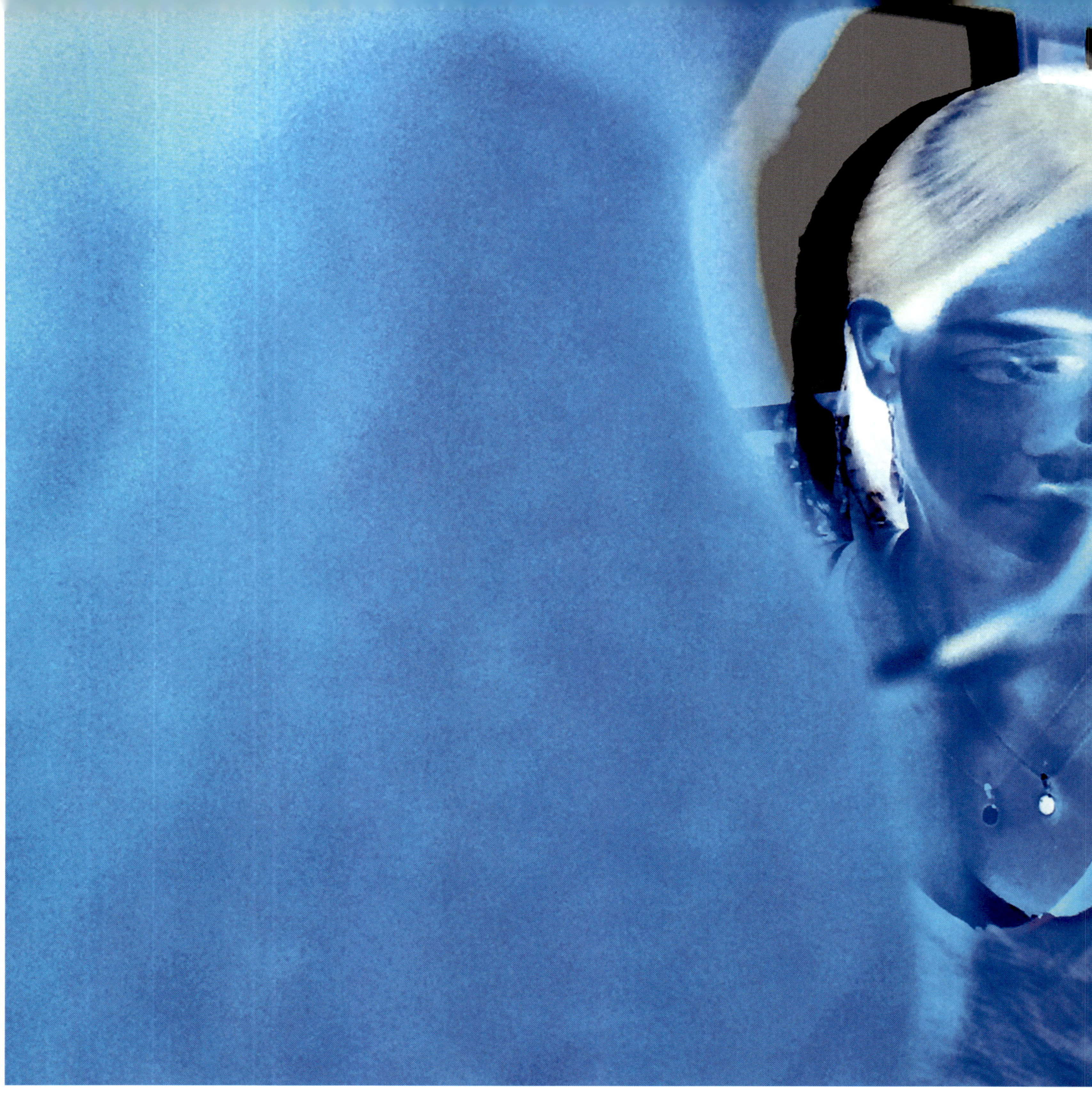

Luisa Blue Duo / São Paulo / 2014

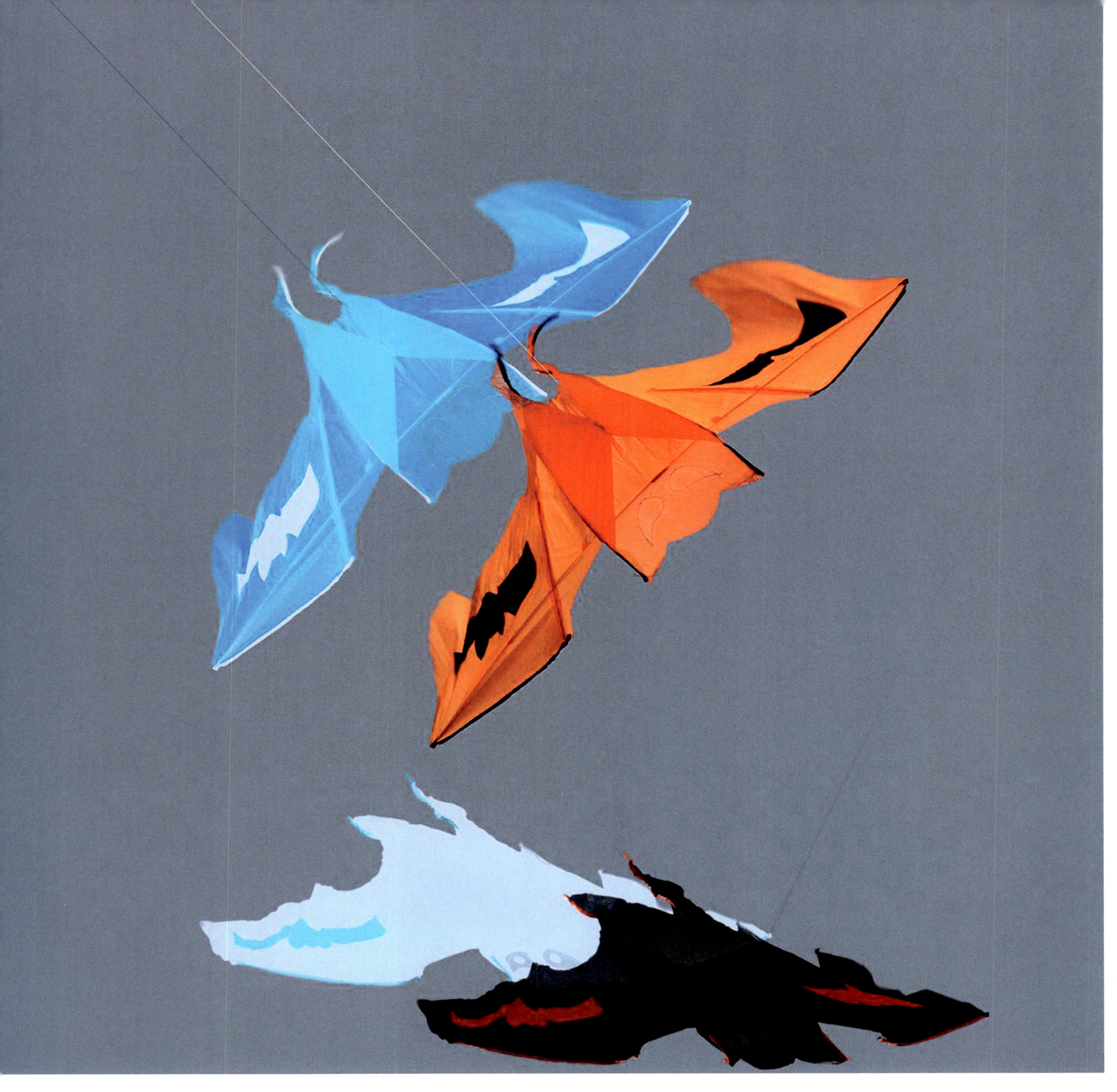

Kites / Rio / 2013

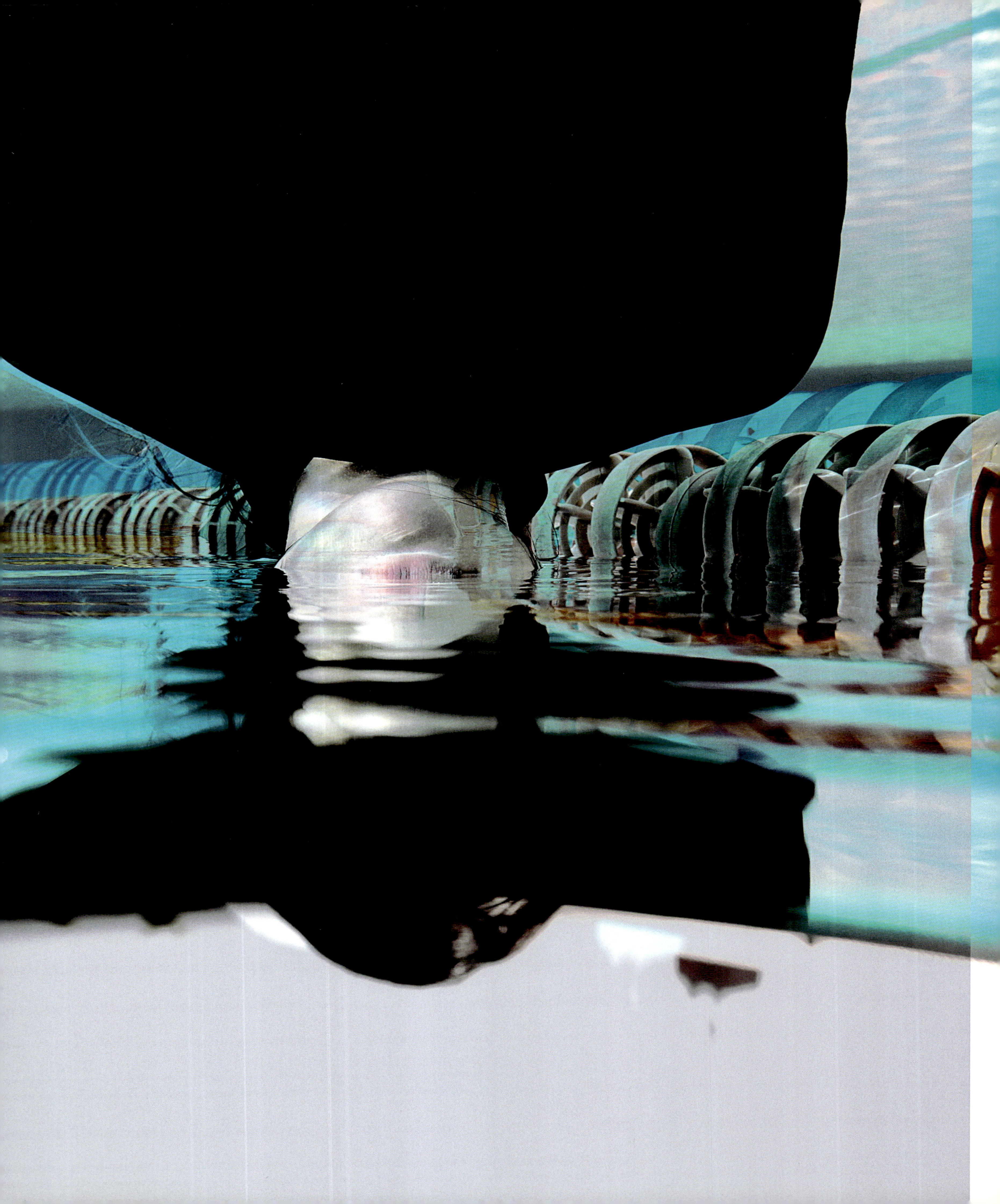

Strange Future / São Paulo / 2014

Lea Duo Black / Jeandelize / 2014

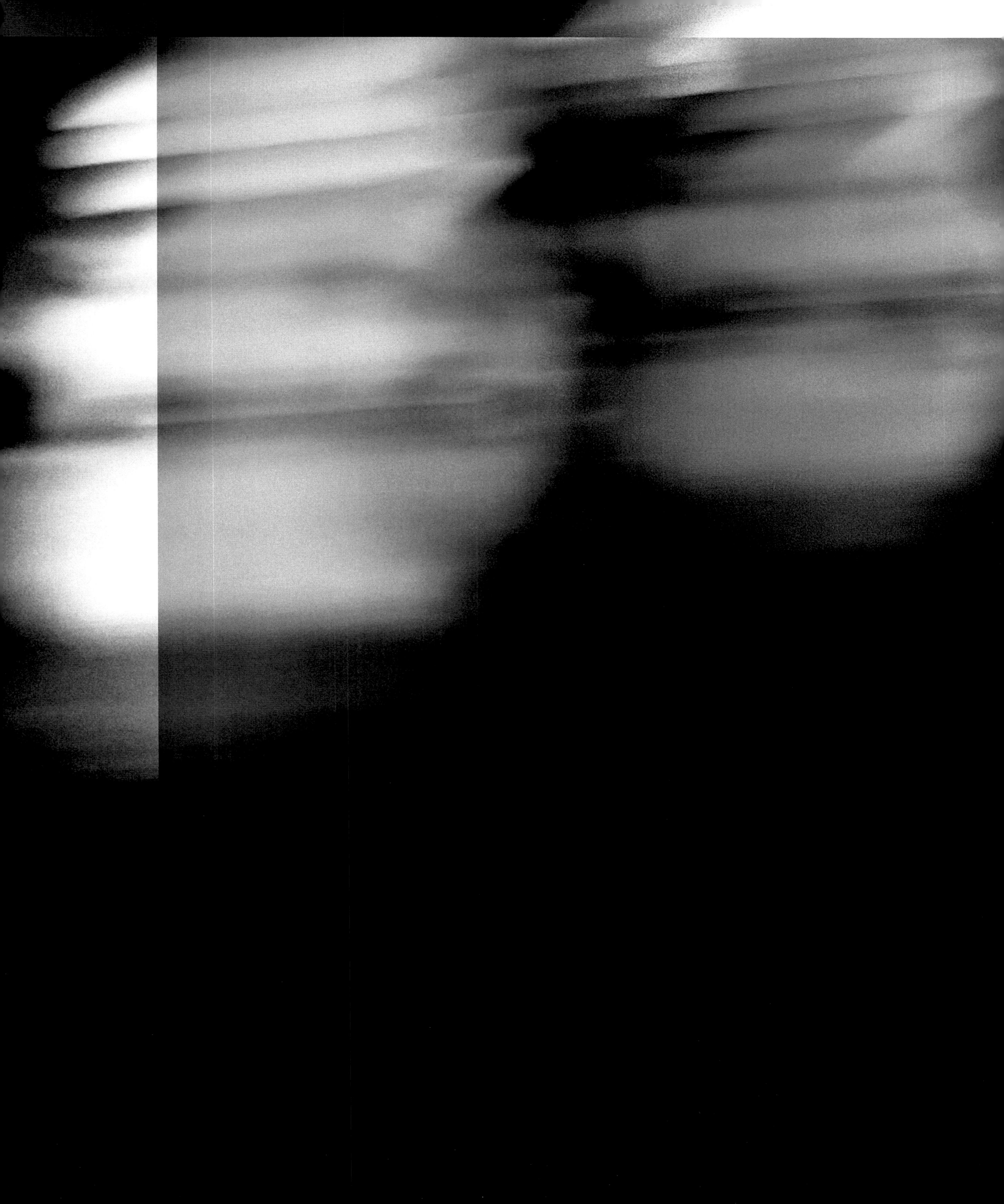

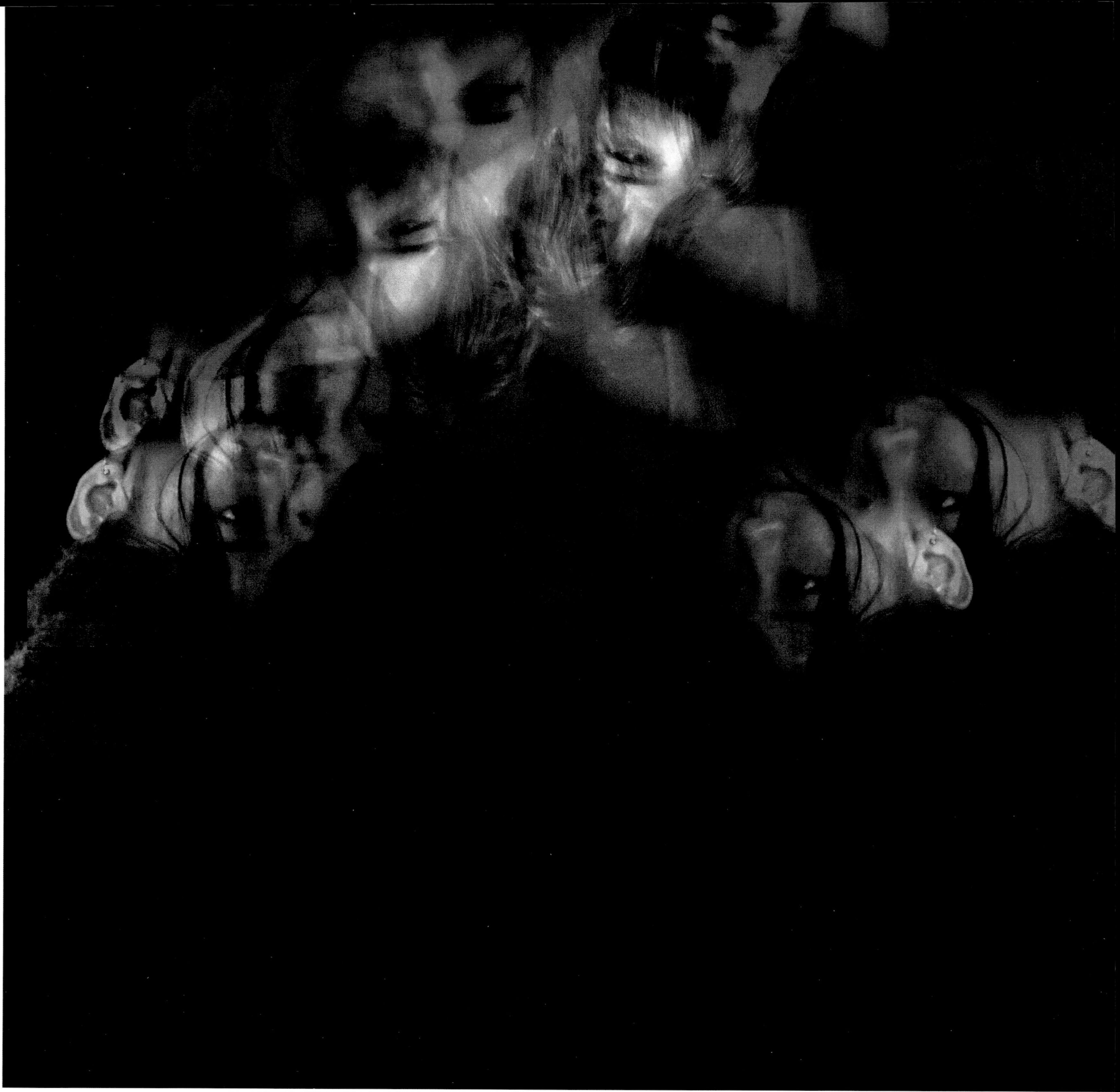

Secret Party Duo / Honolulu / 2014

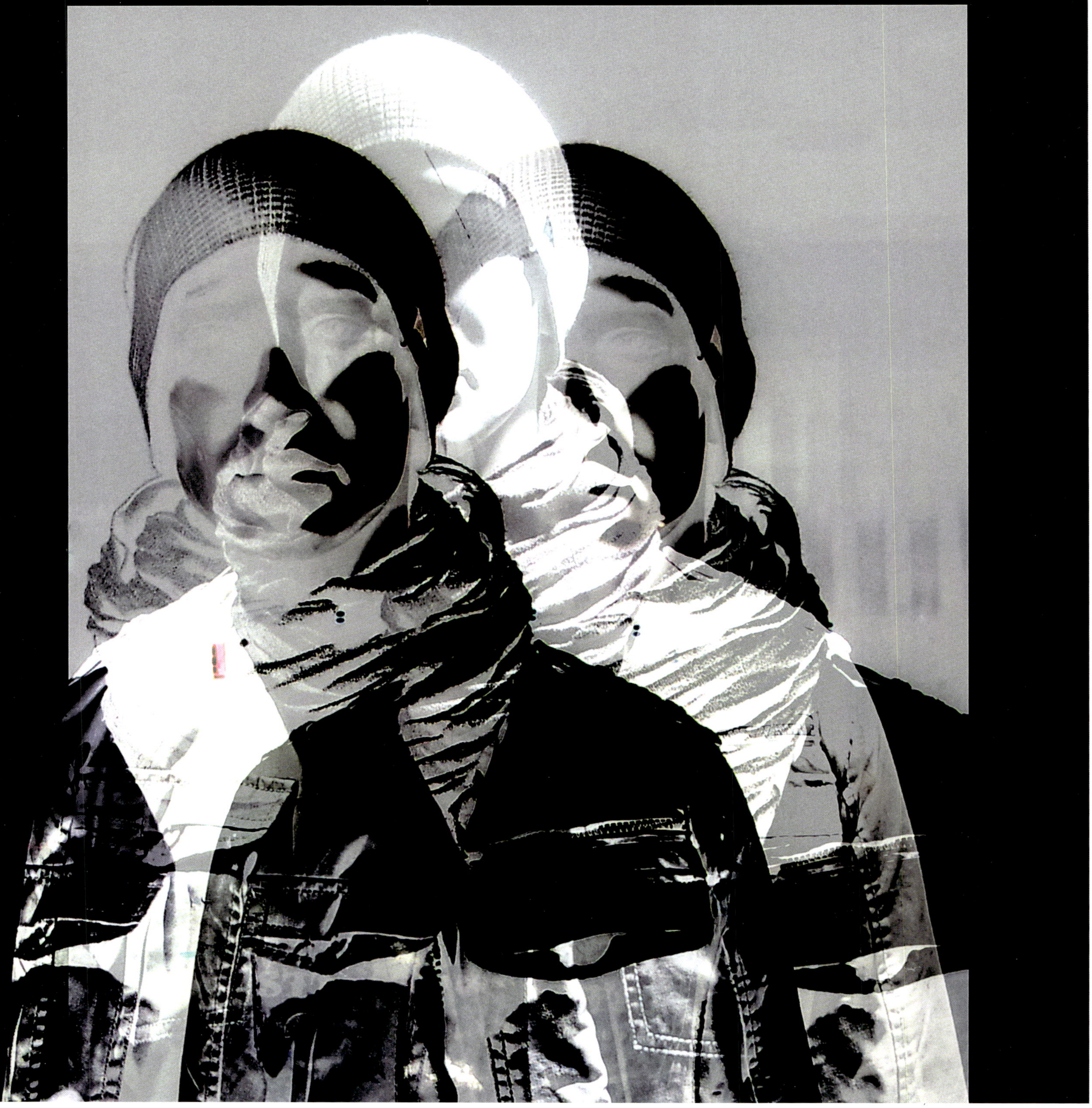

Warriors Duo / Berlin / 2012

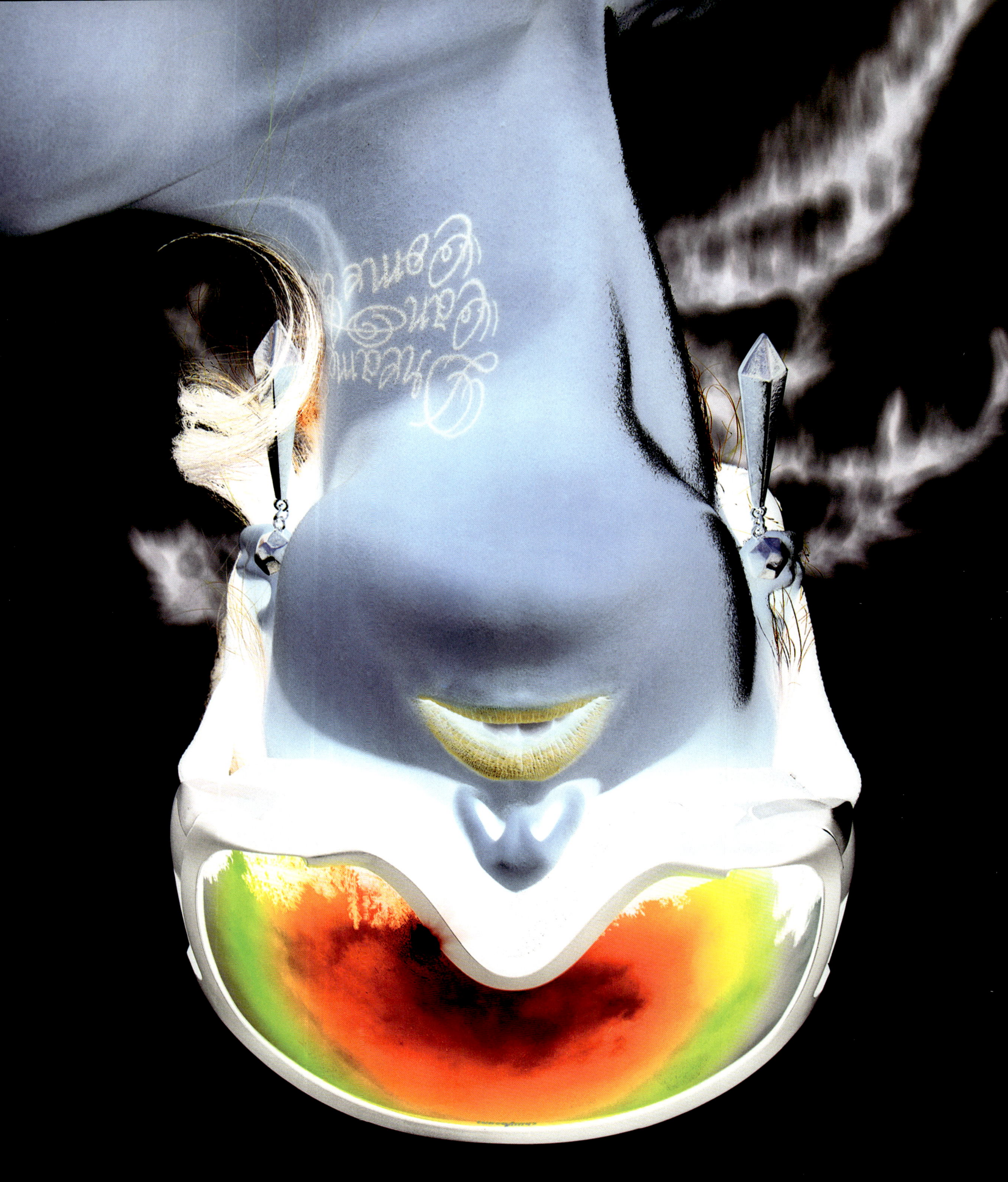

Tati Invert / São Paulo / 2015

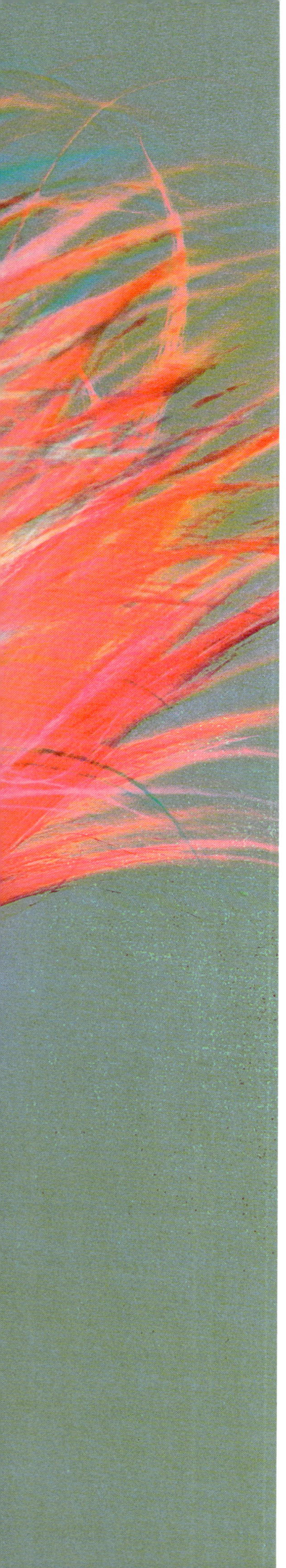

Tati Tricolore Duo / São Paulo / 2015

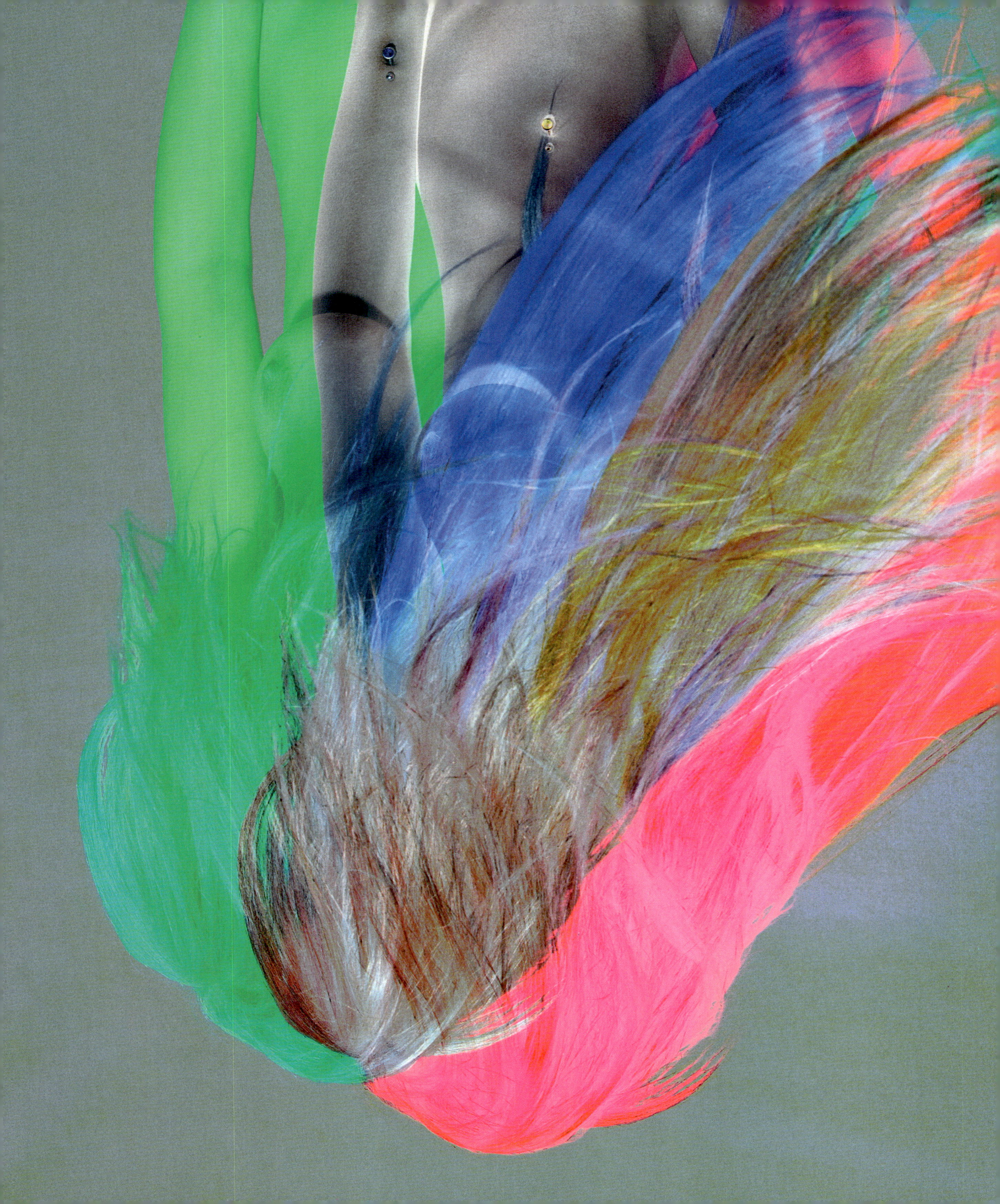

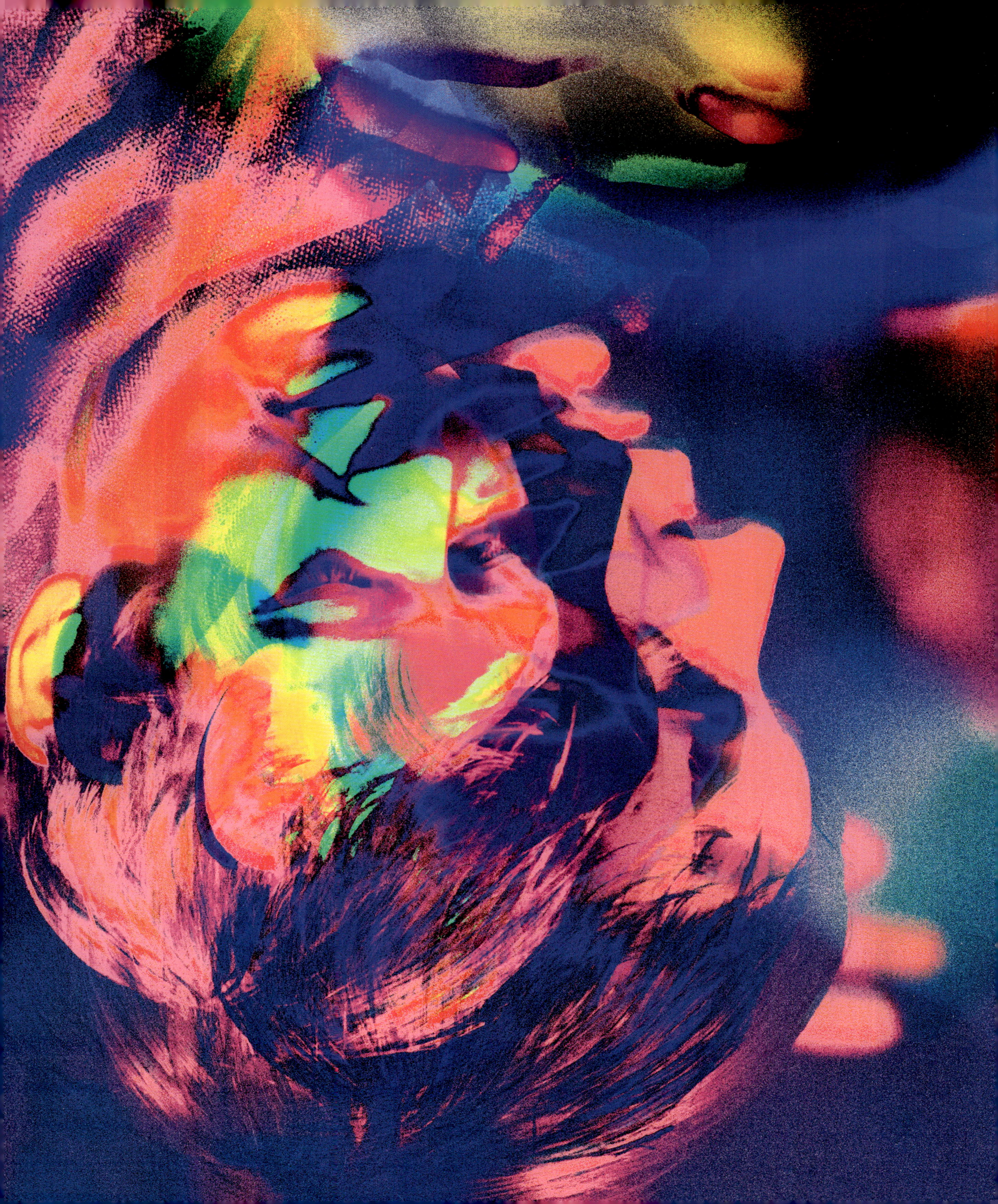

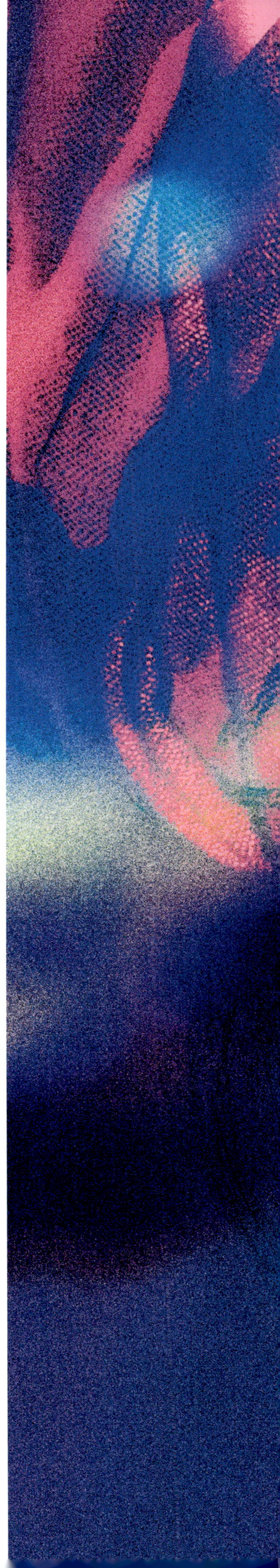

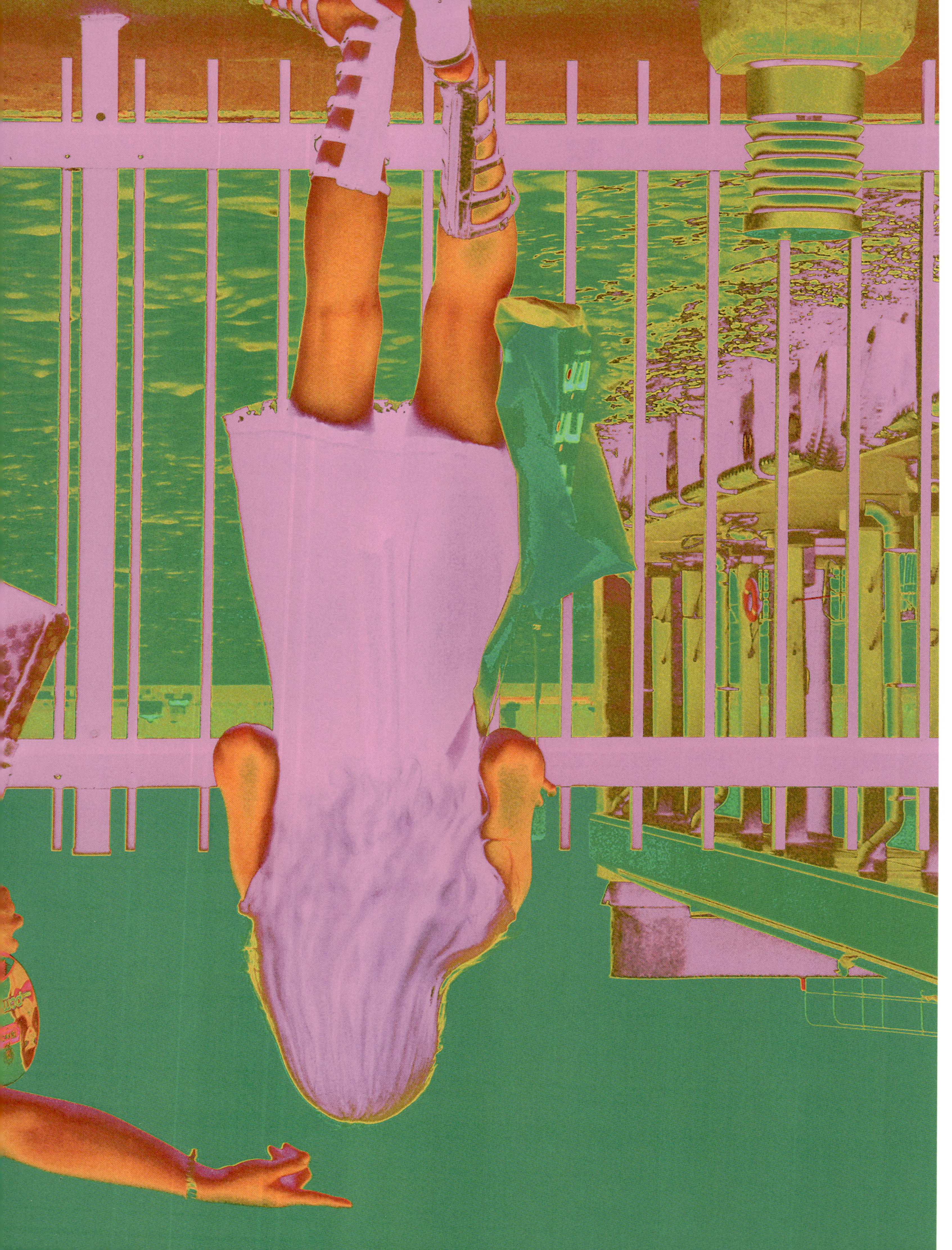

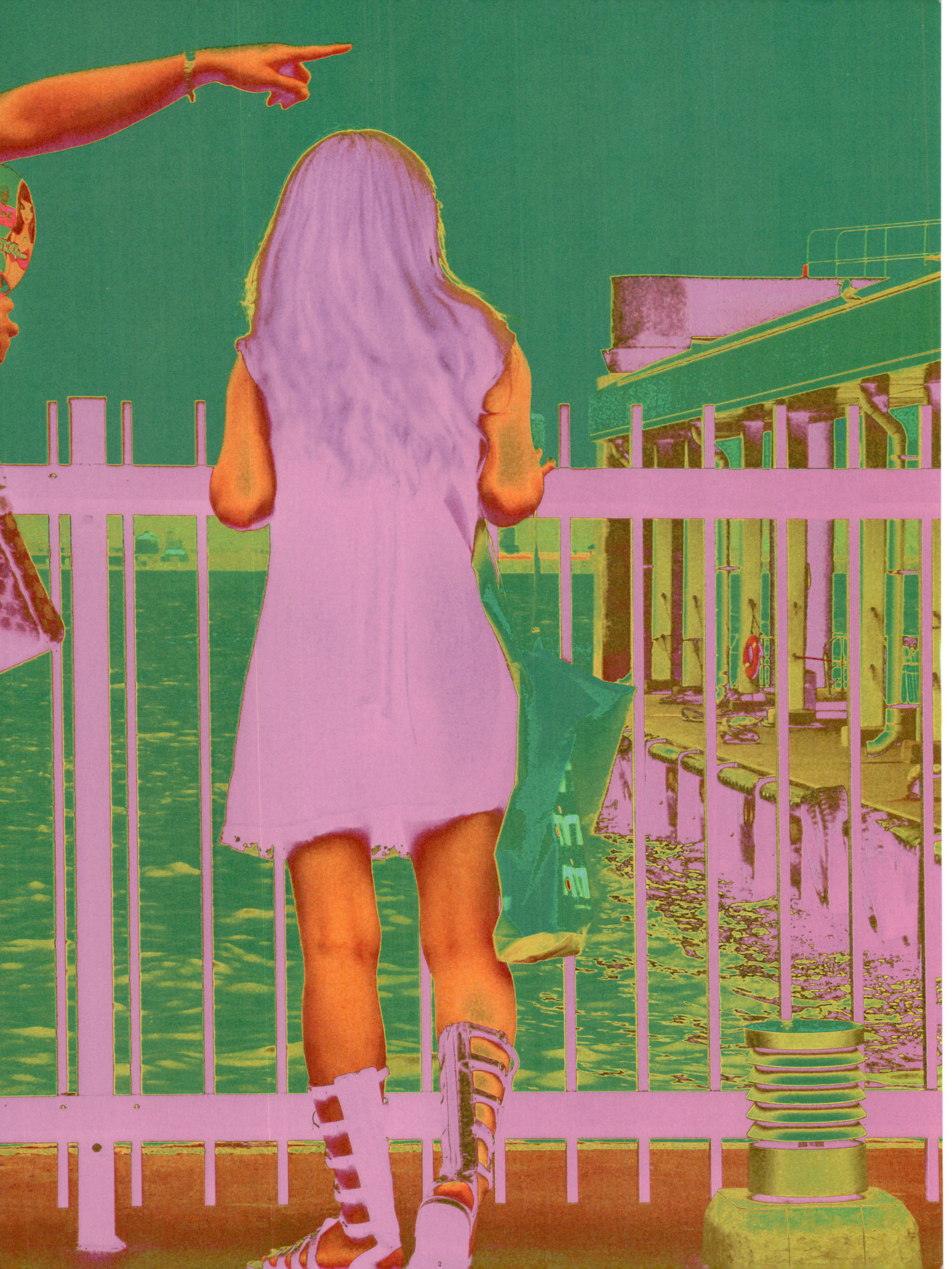

Tokyo Girls Pink Duo Acid / Tokyo / 2008

Fashion Duo / Paris / 2014

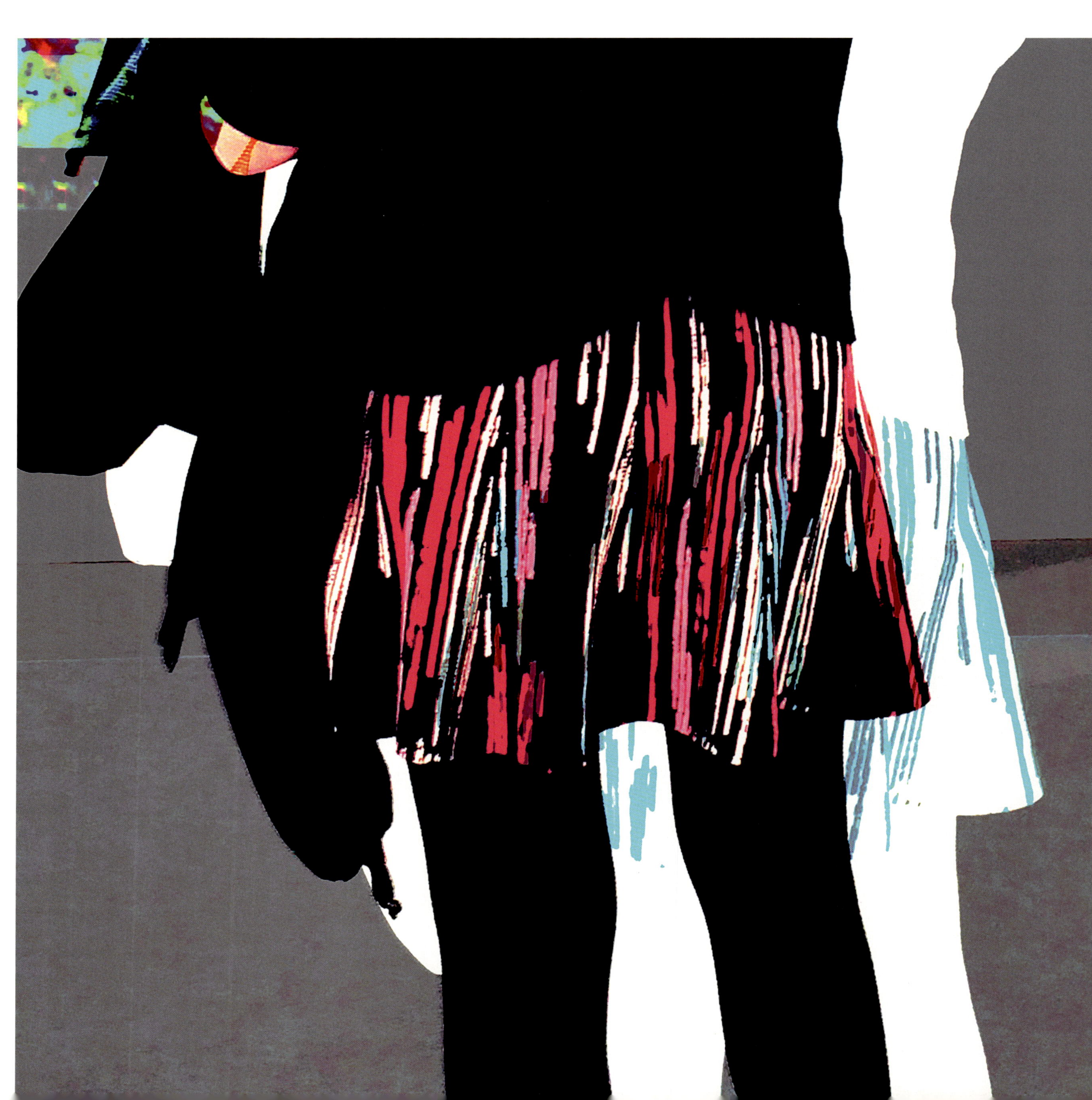

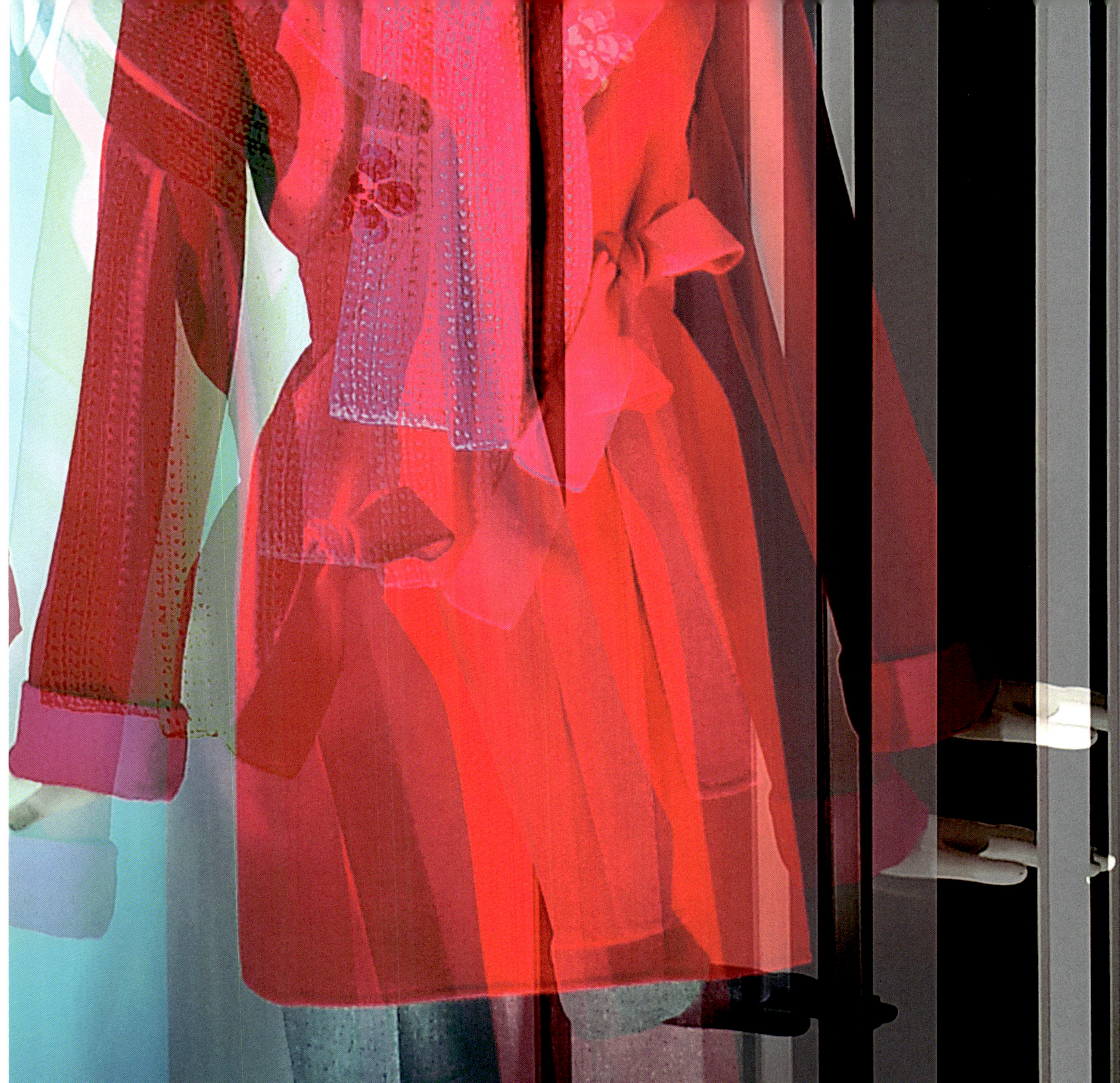

Taylor Duo / Milan / 2012

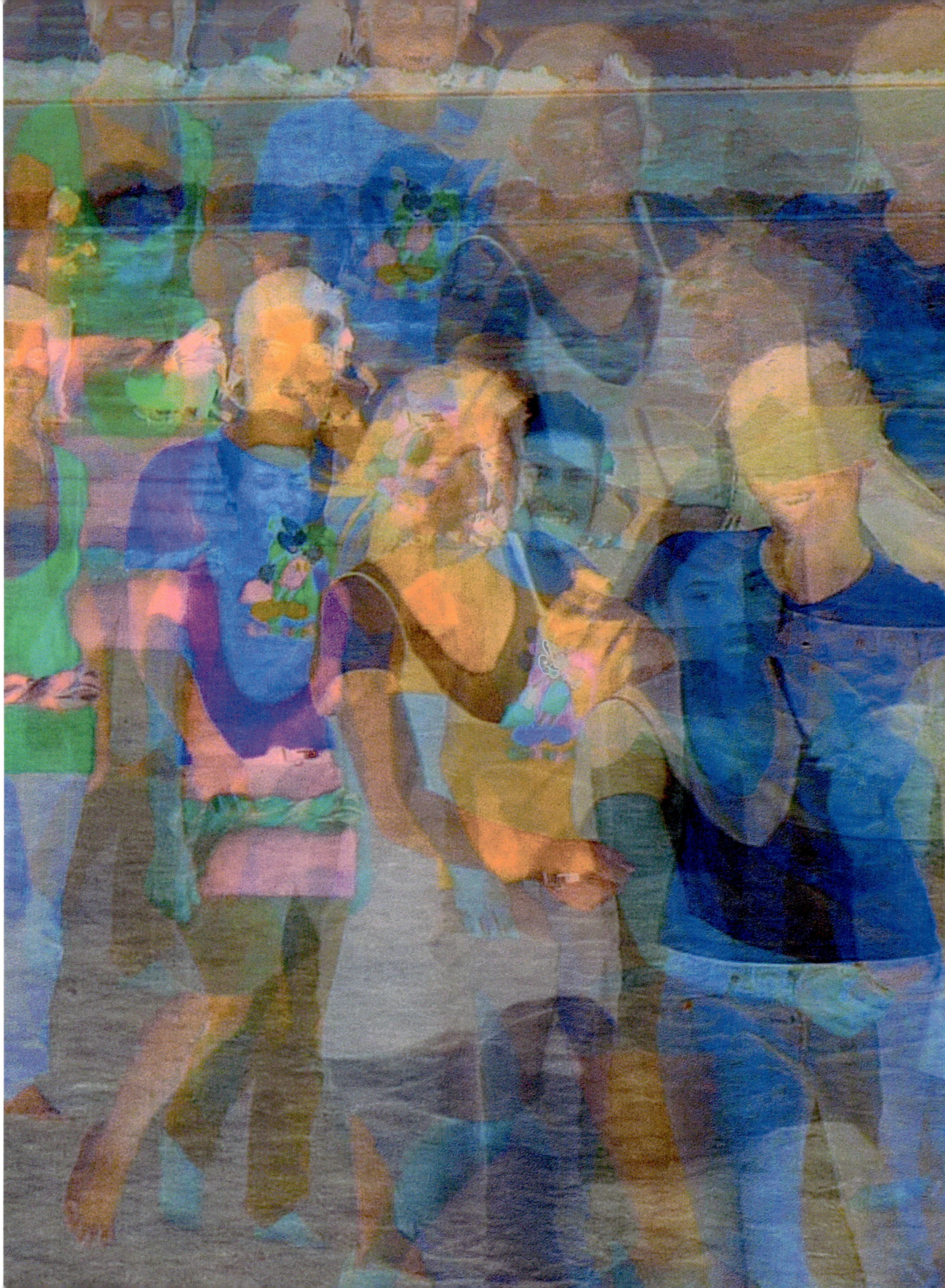

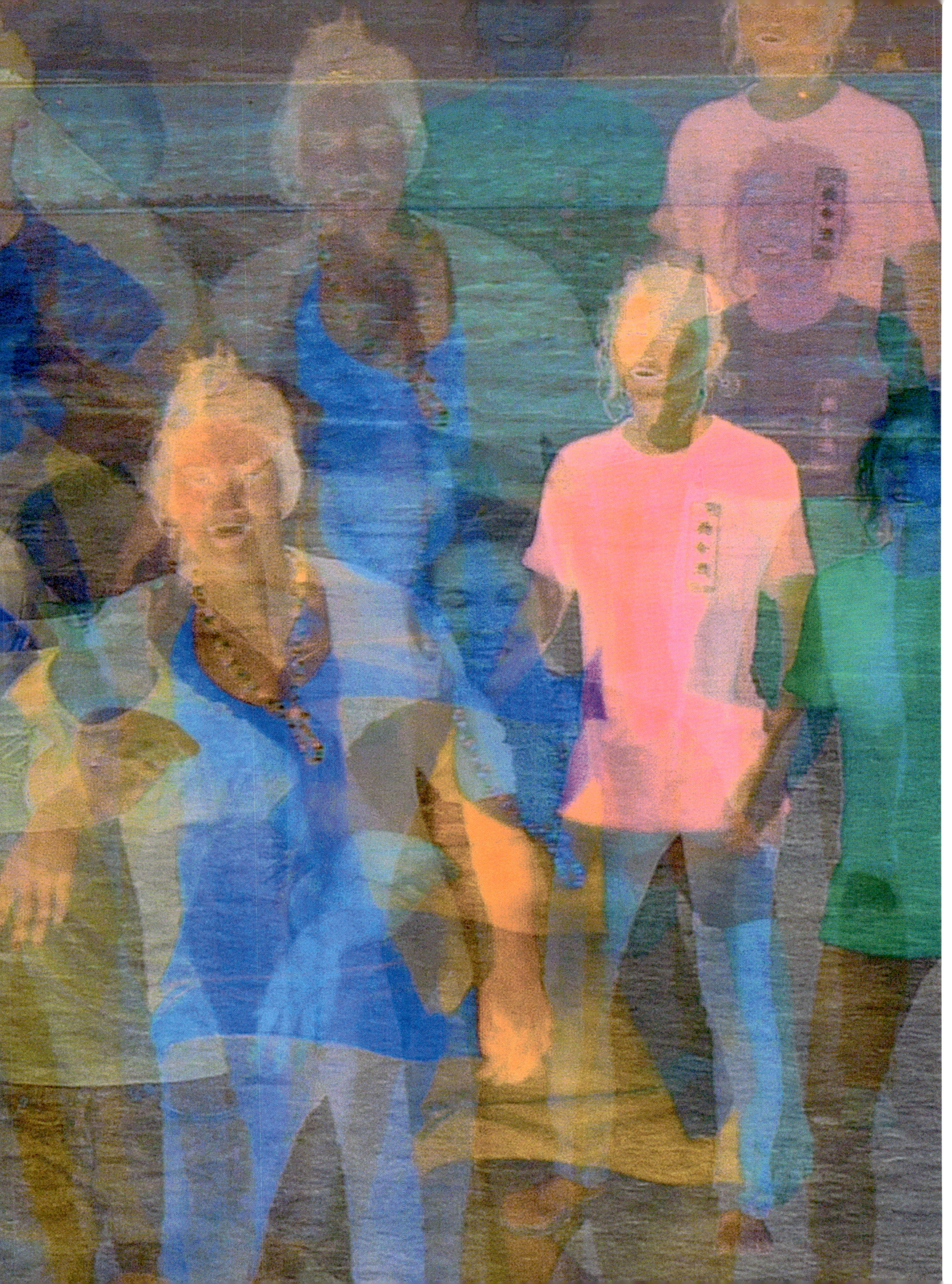

Cabra Cega / Lido / 2009

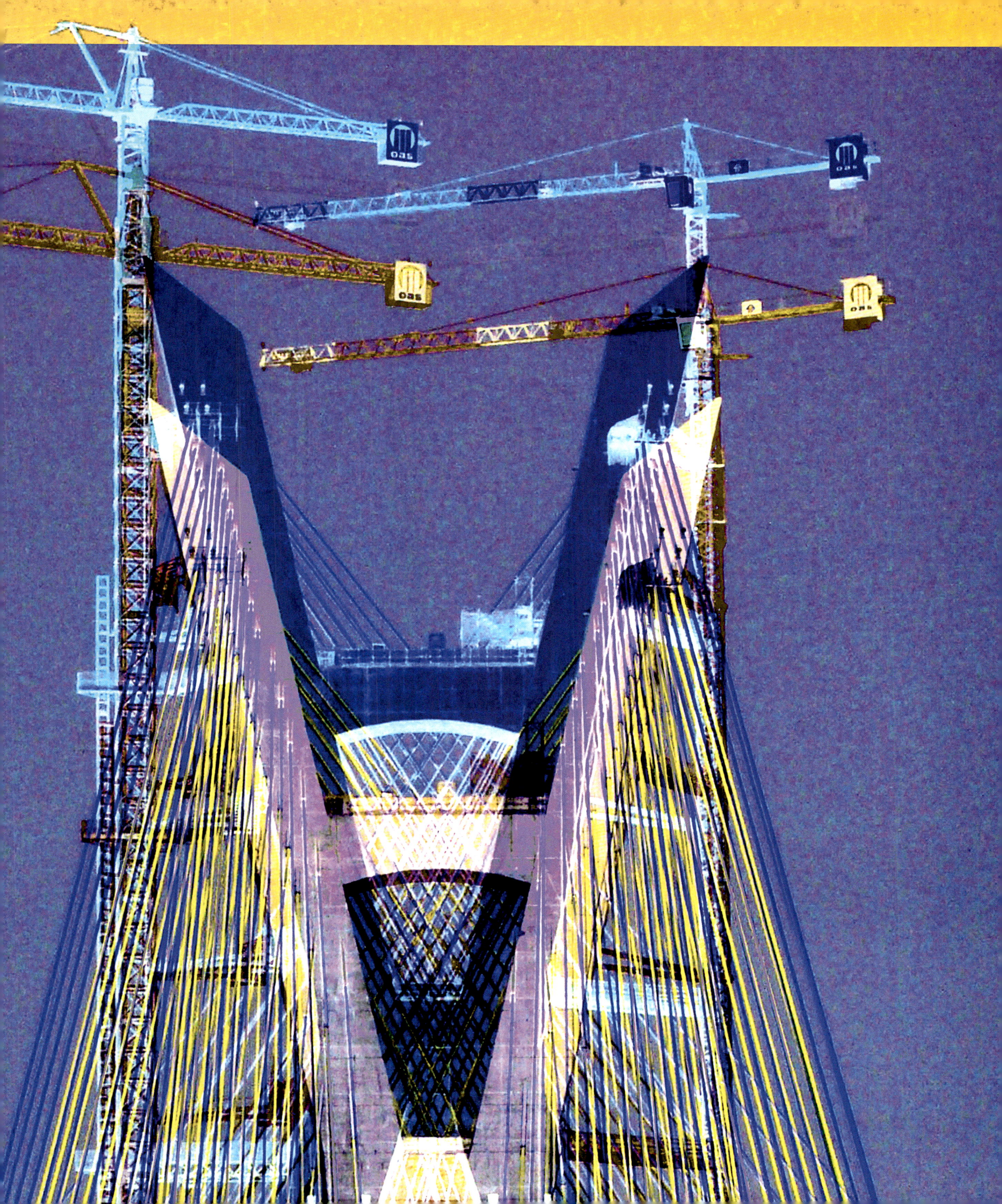

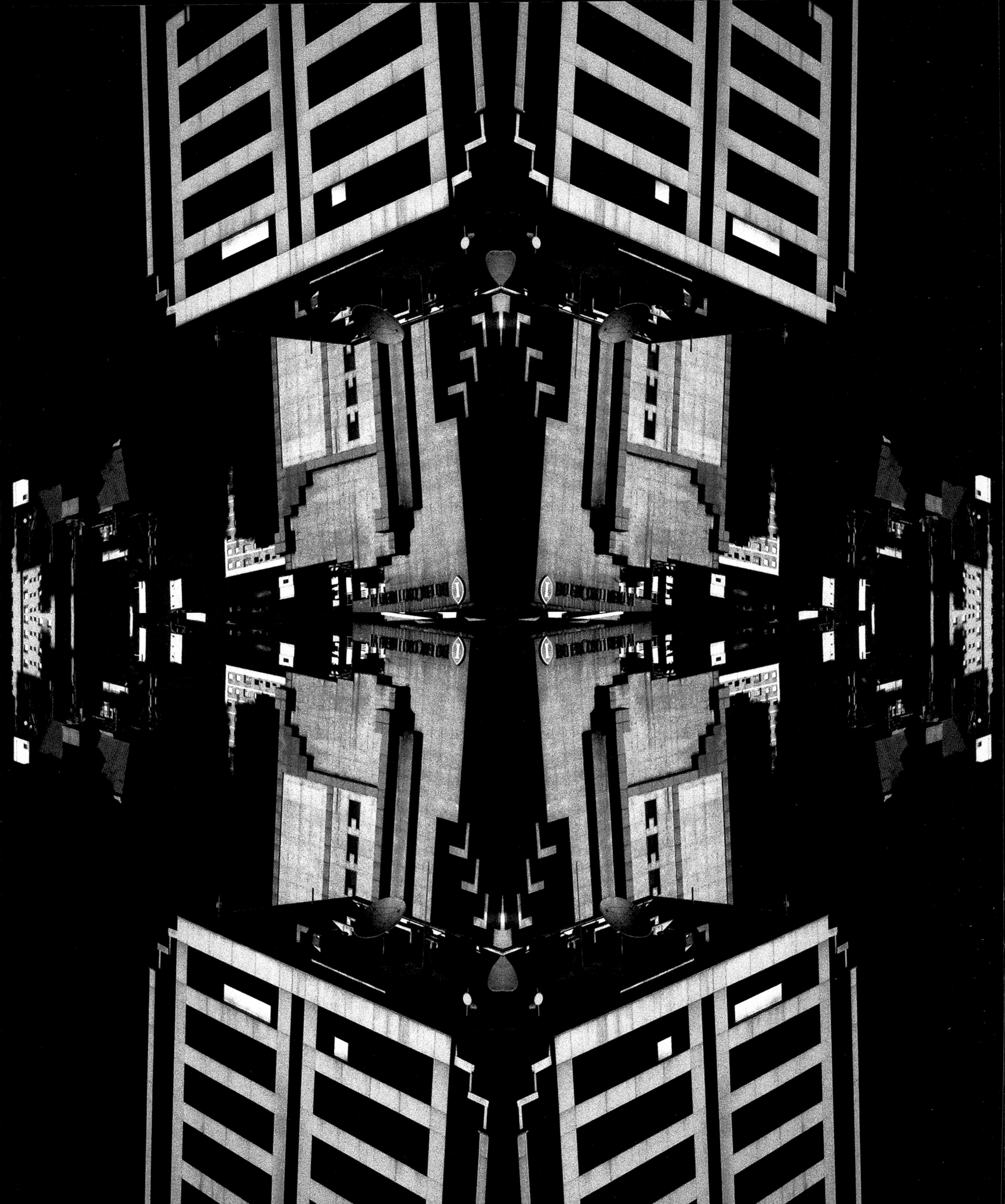

A Cidade Que Cai I / São Paulo / 2012

A Cidade Que Cai II / São Paulo / 2012

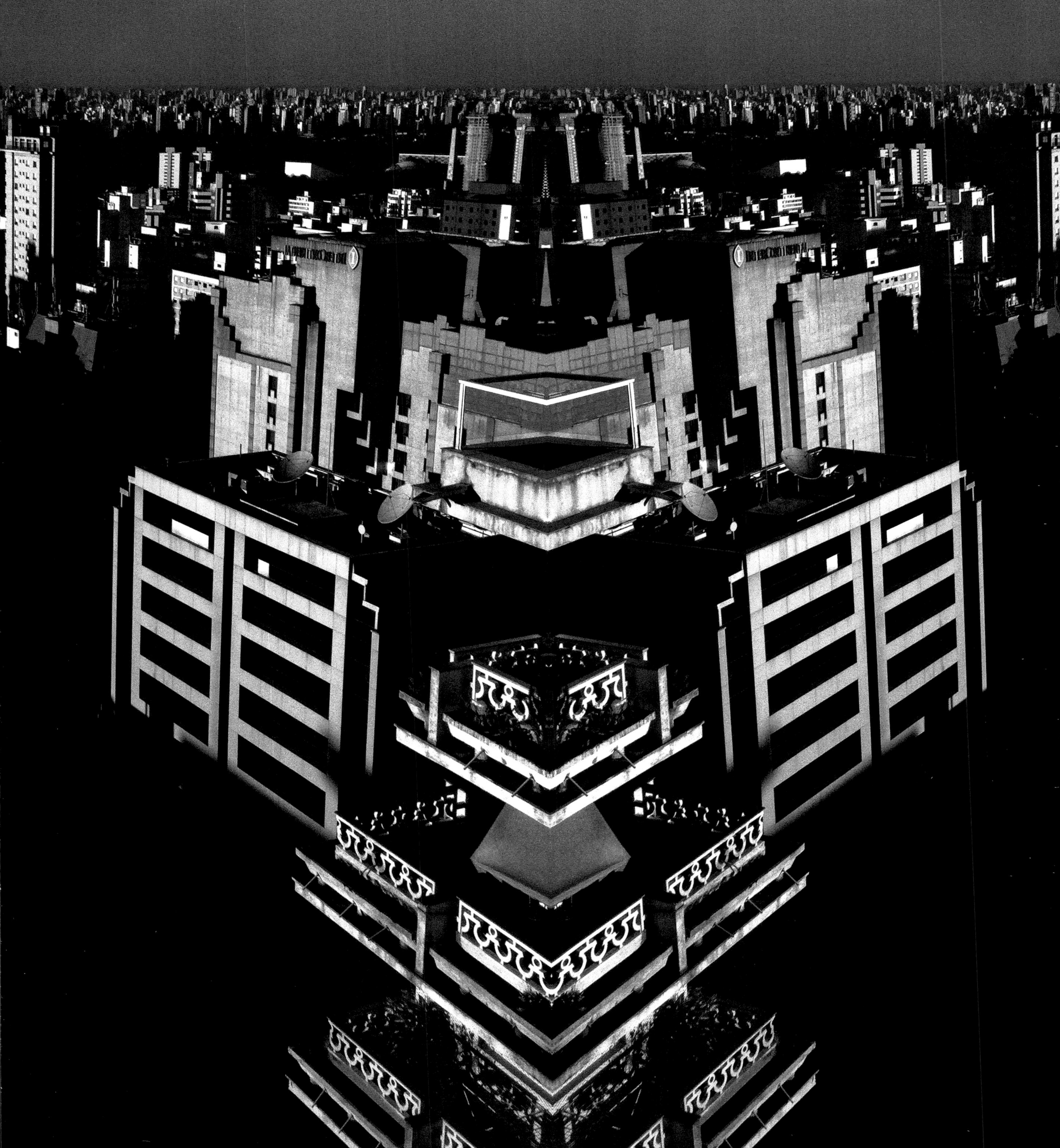

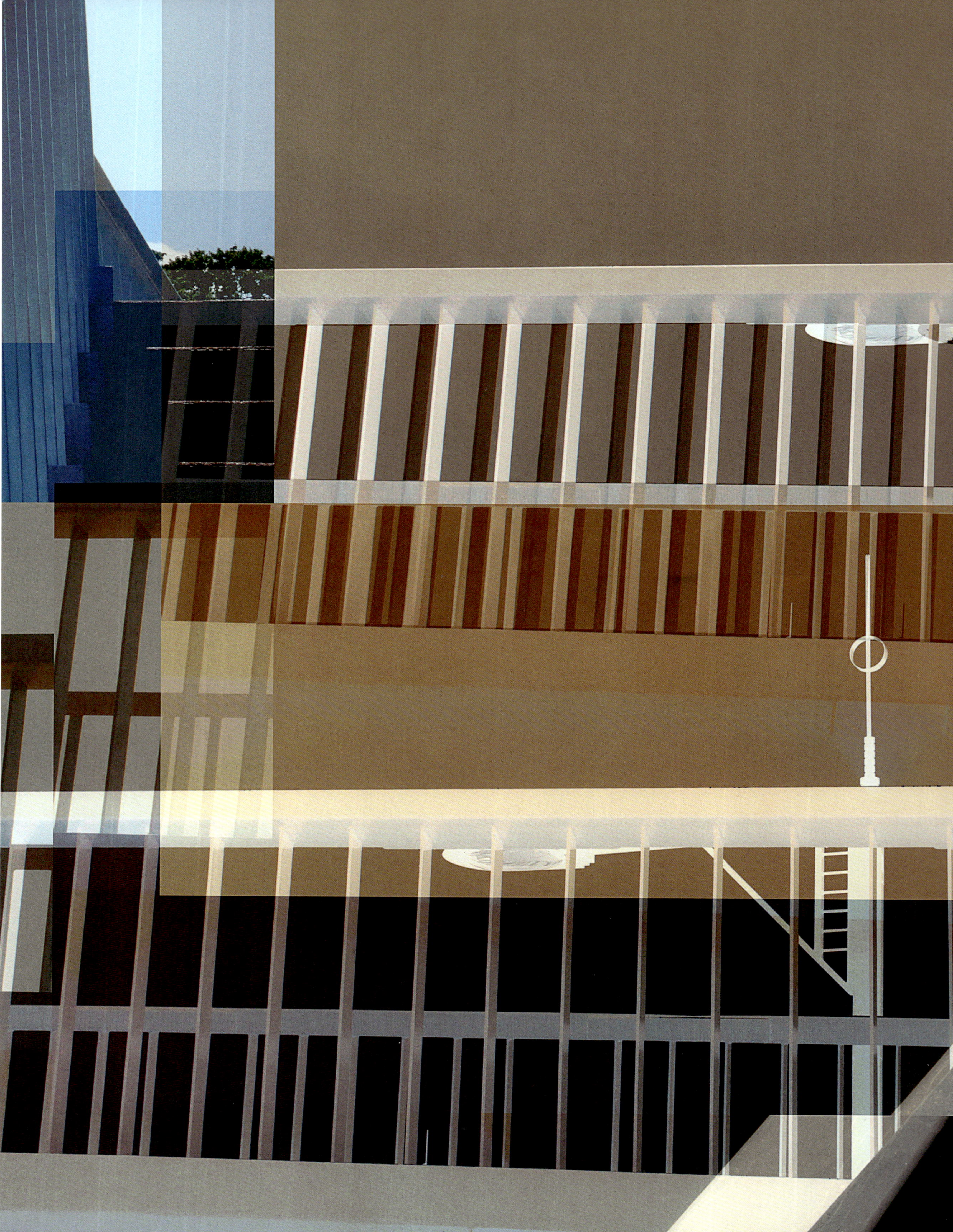

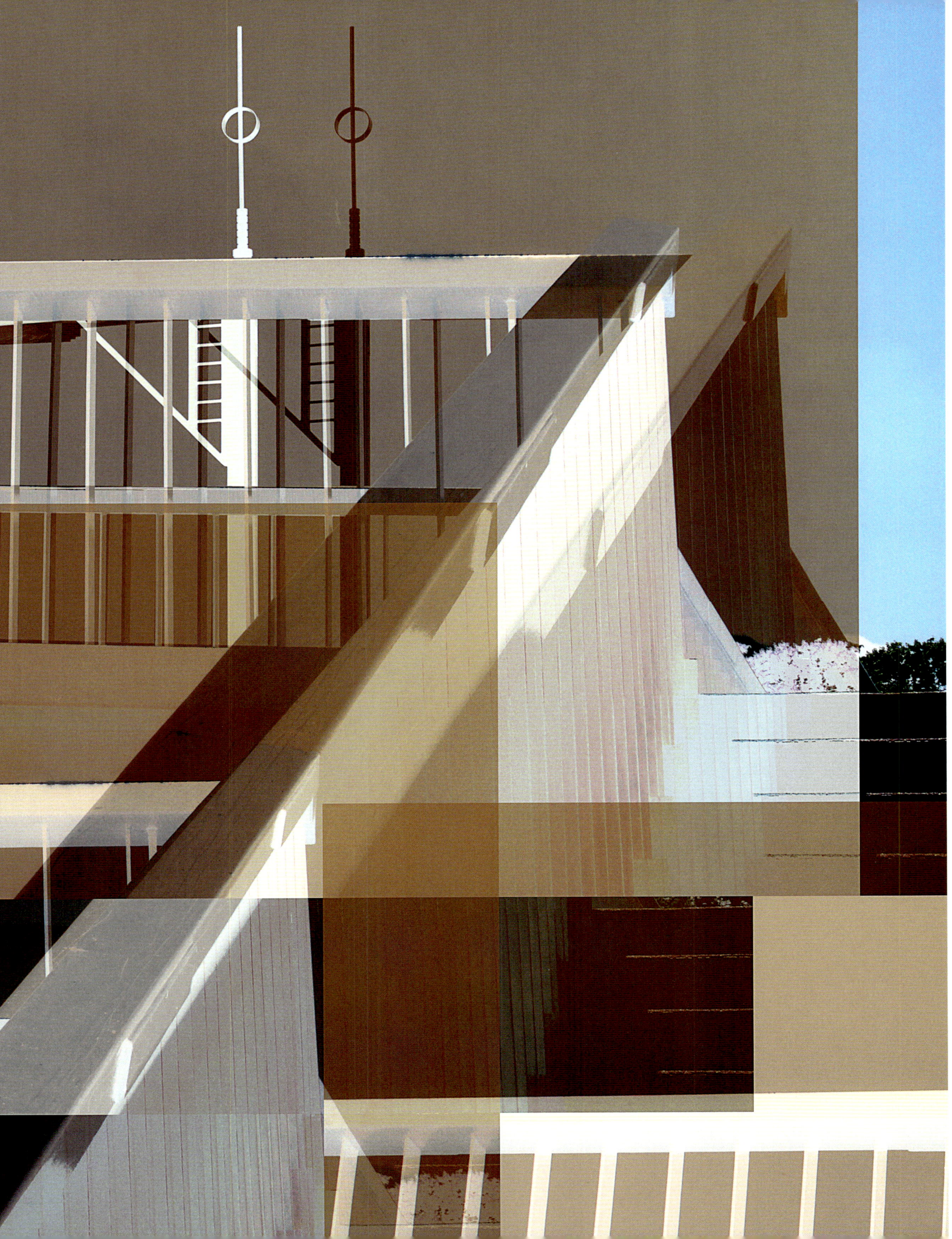

Tokyo Bridges Duo / Tokyo / 2008

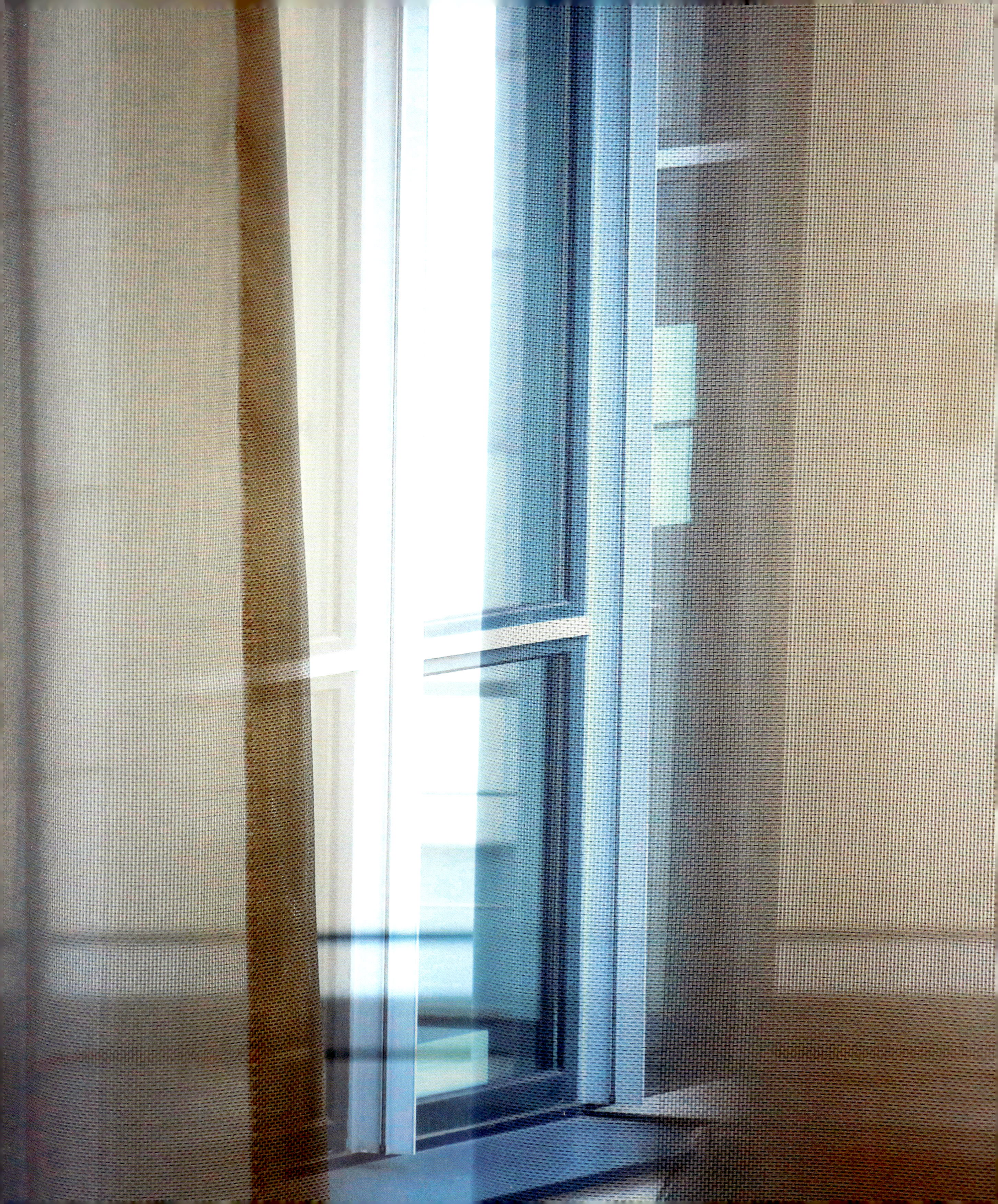

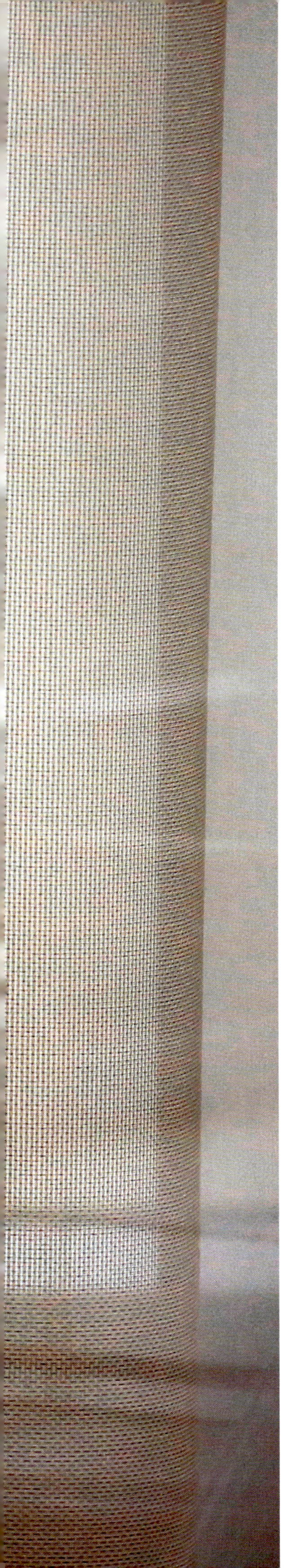

Berlin Window Duo / Berlin / 2012

Die Überfahrt / Jeandelize / 2015

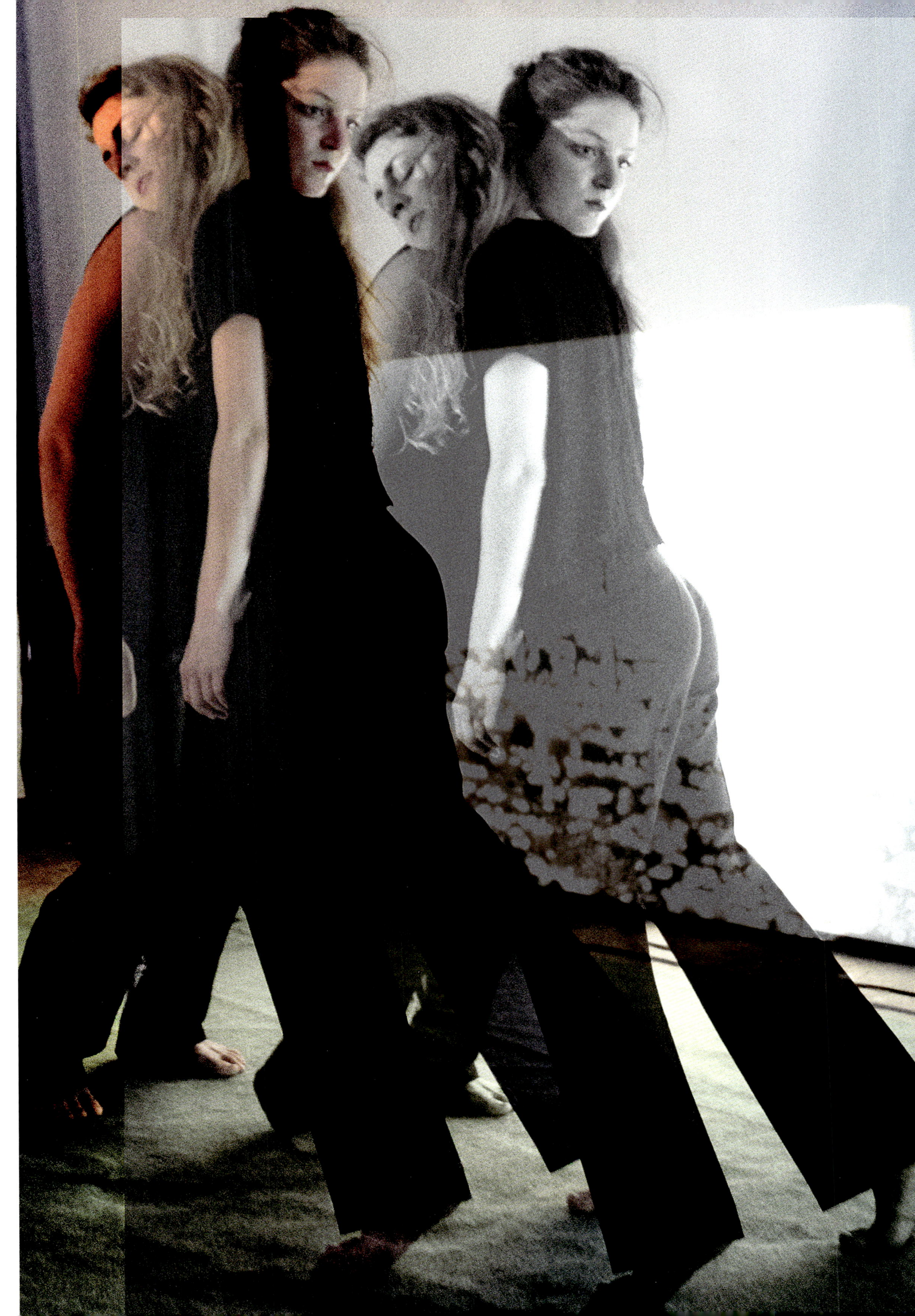

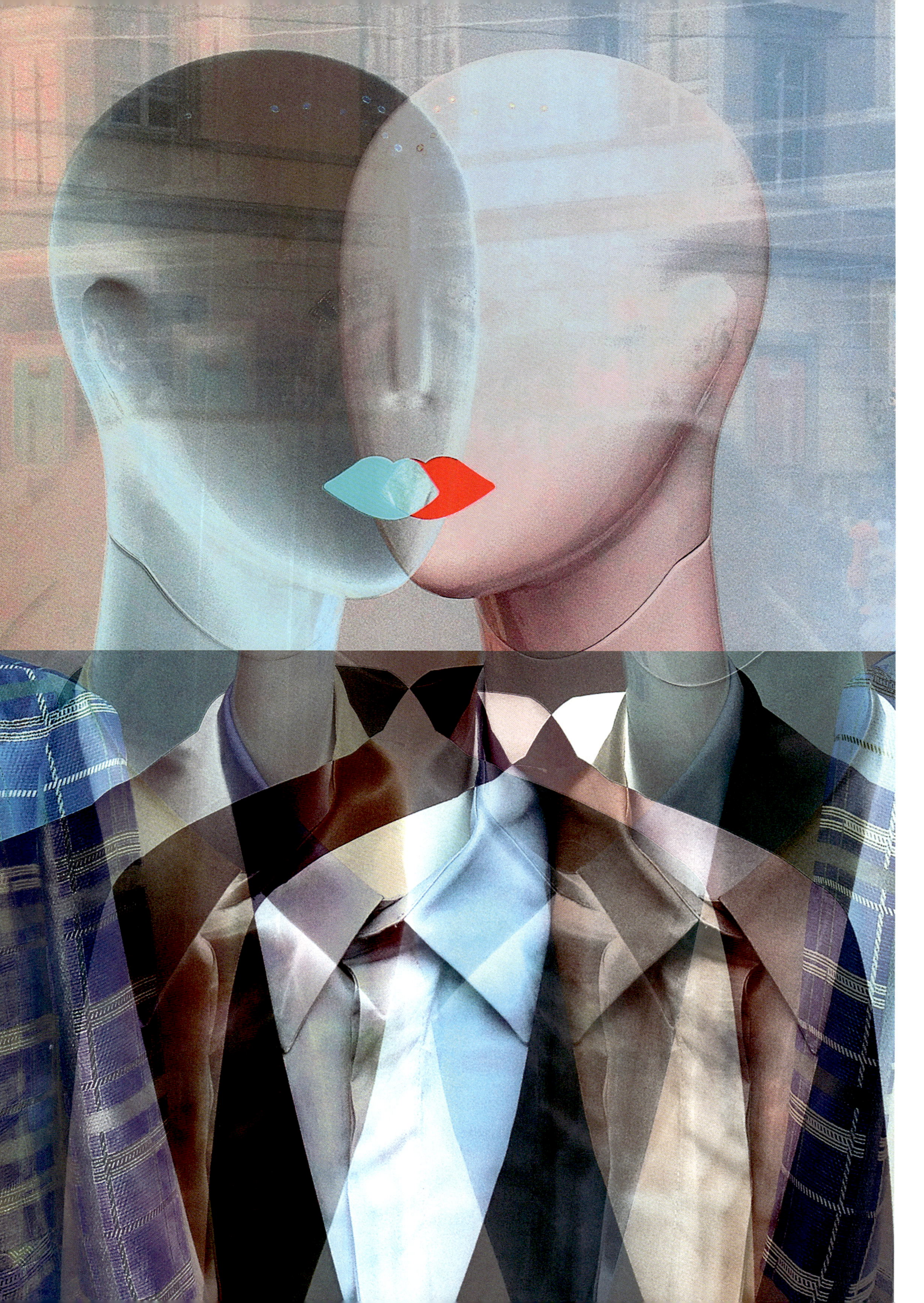

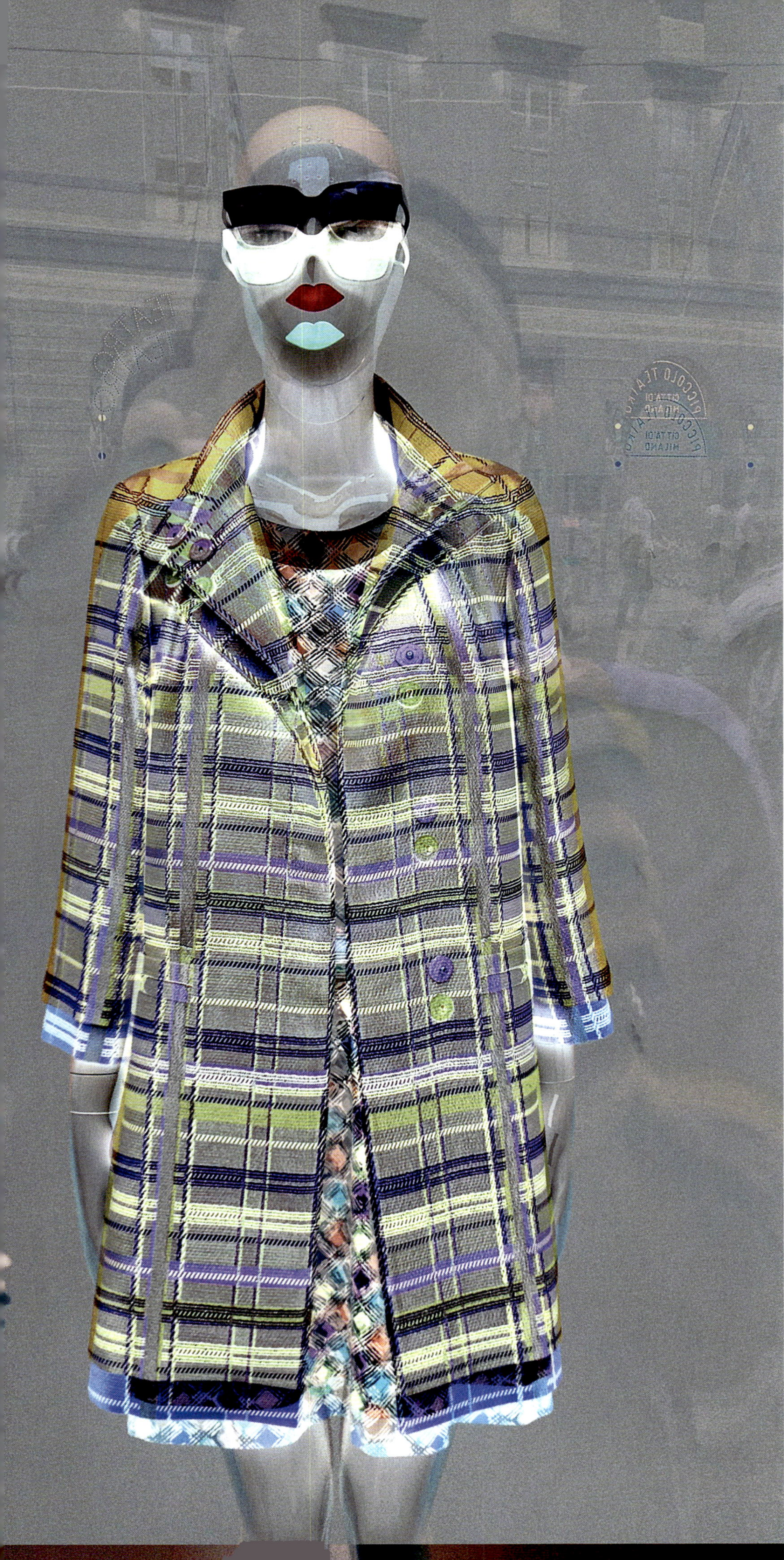

Long Woman / Milan / 2013

Venezia Mannequin Duo II / Venice / 2009

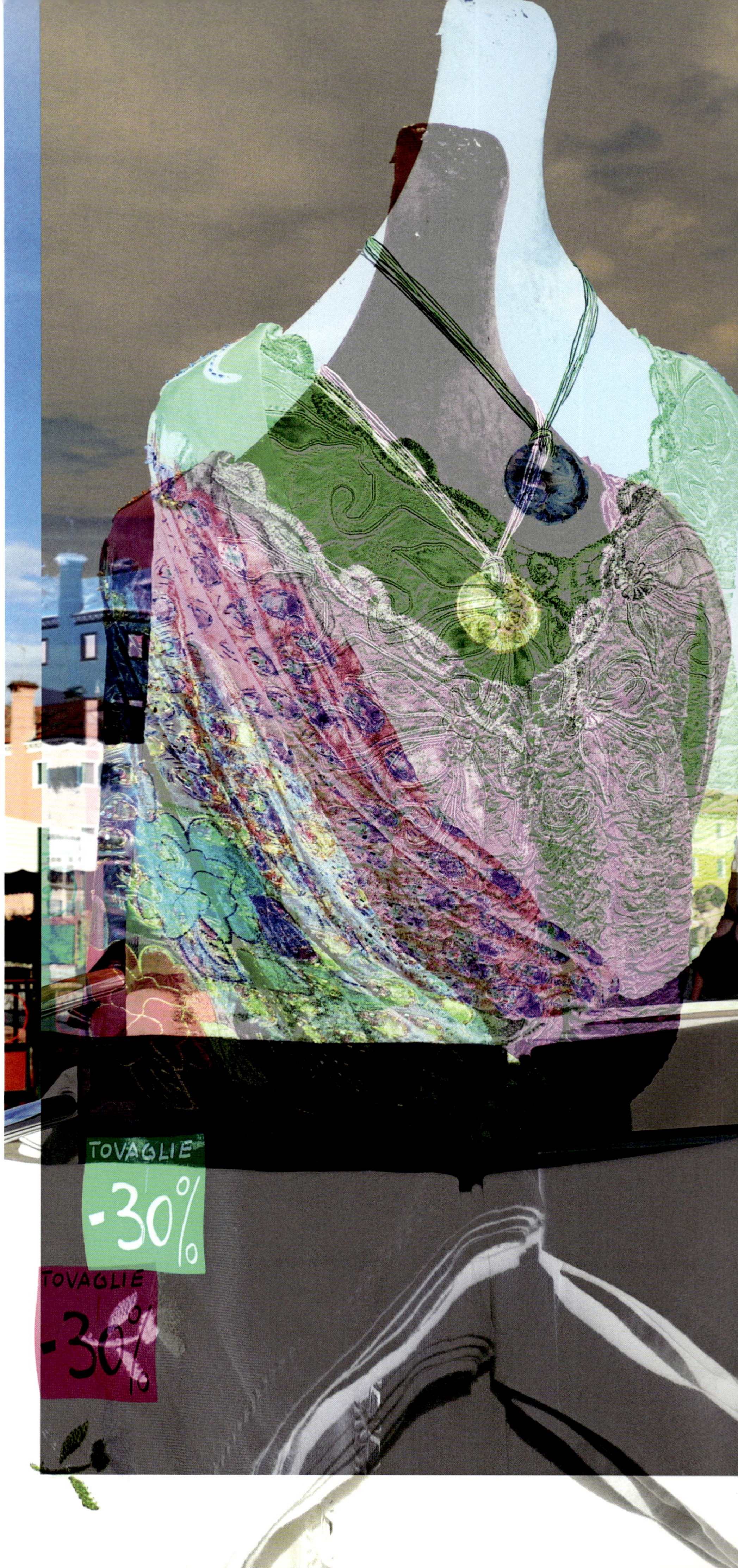
TOVAGLIE
-30%
TOVAGLIE
-30%

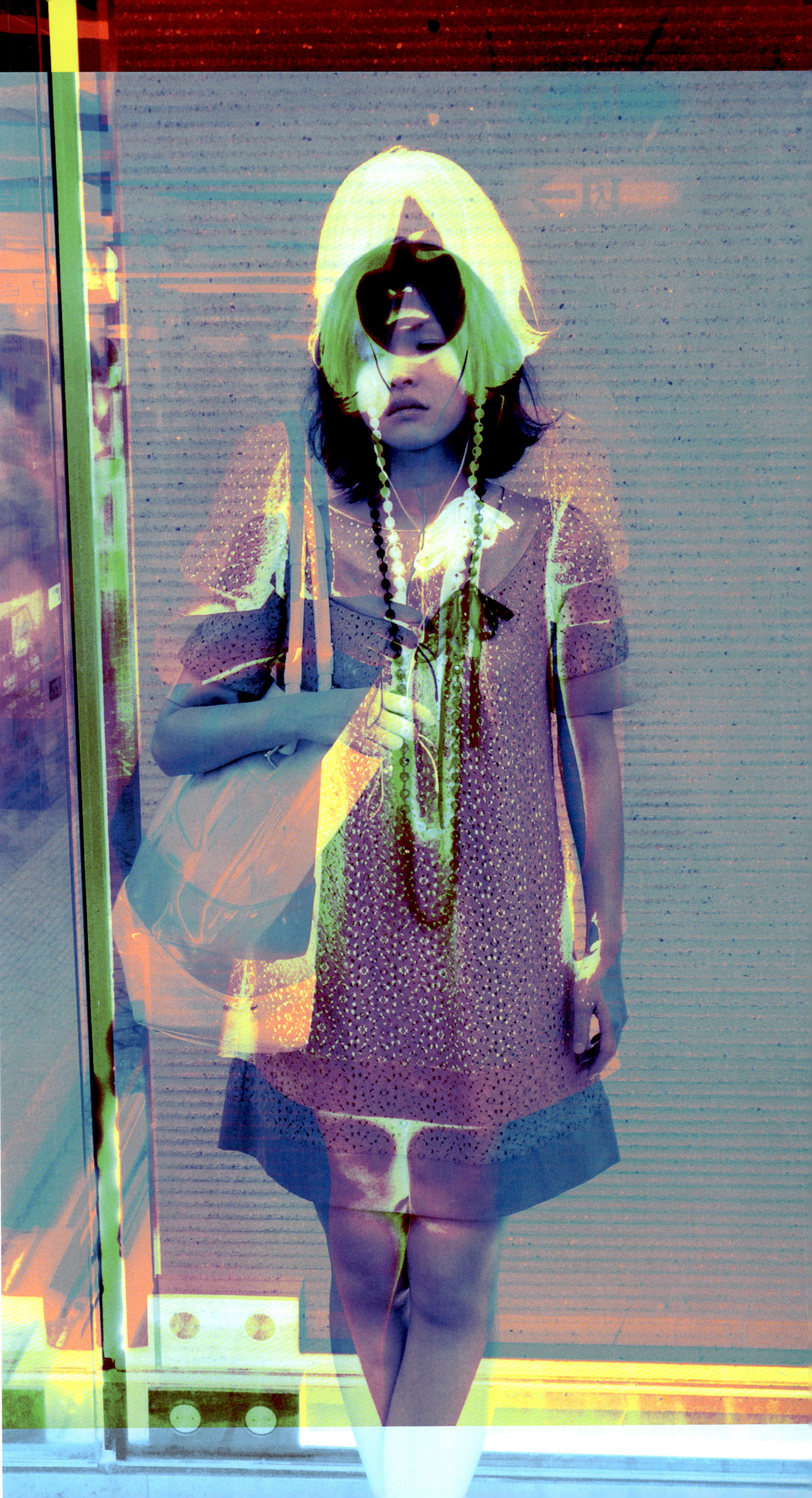

Tokyo Girl Inverted / Tokyo / 2008

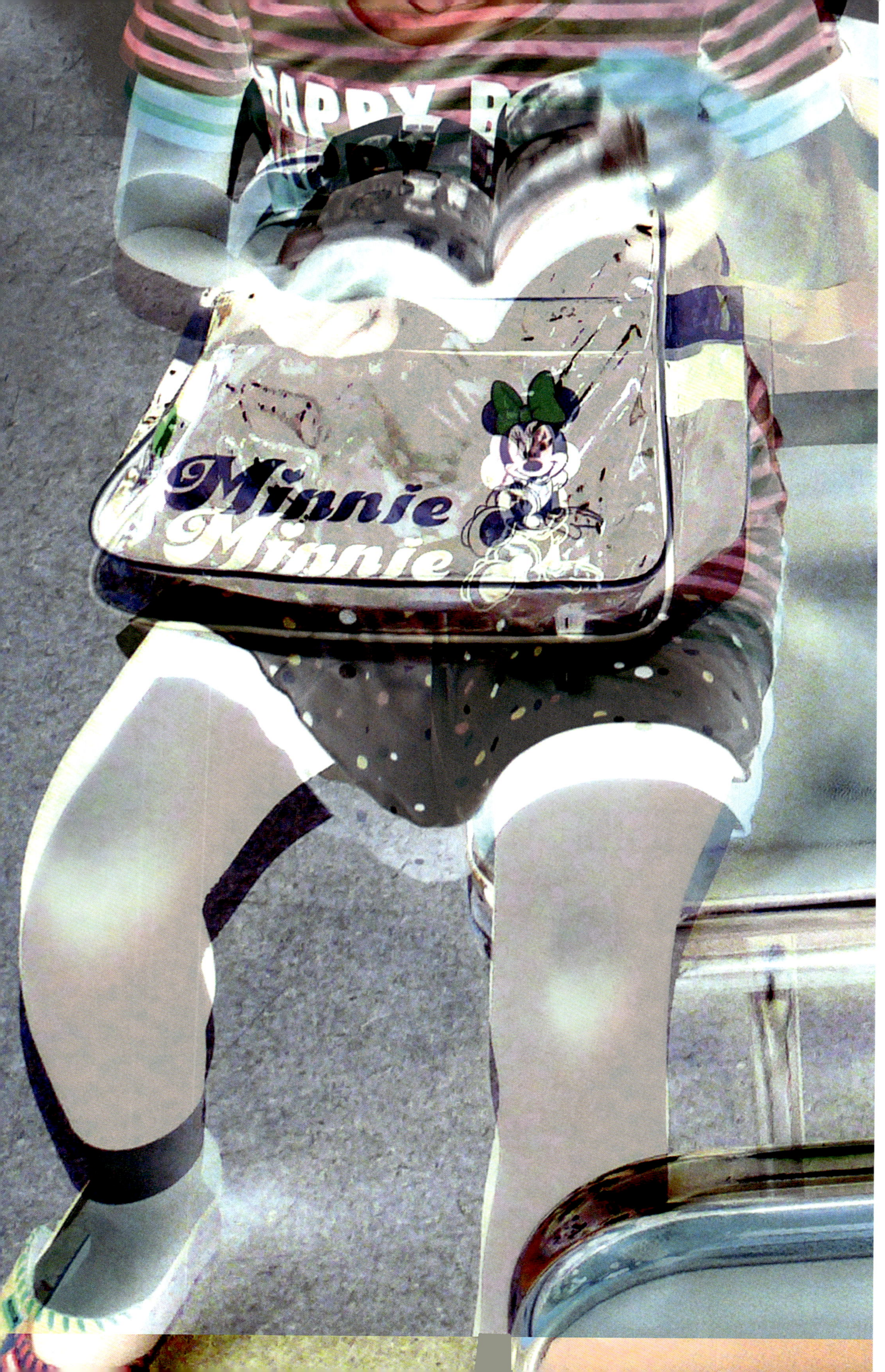

Girl Reading Duo / Tokyo / 2008

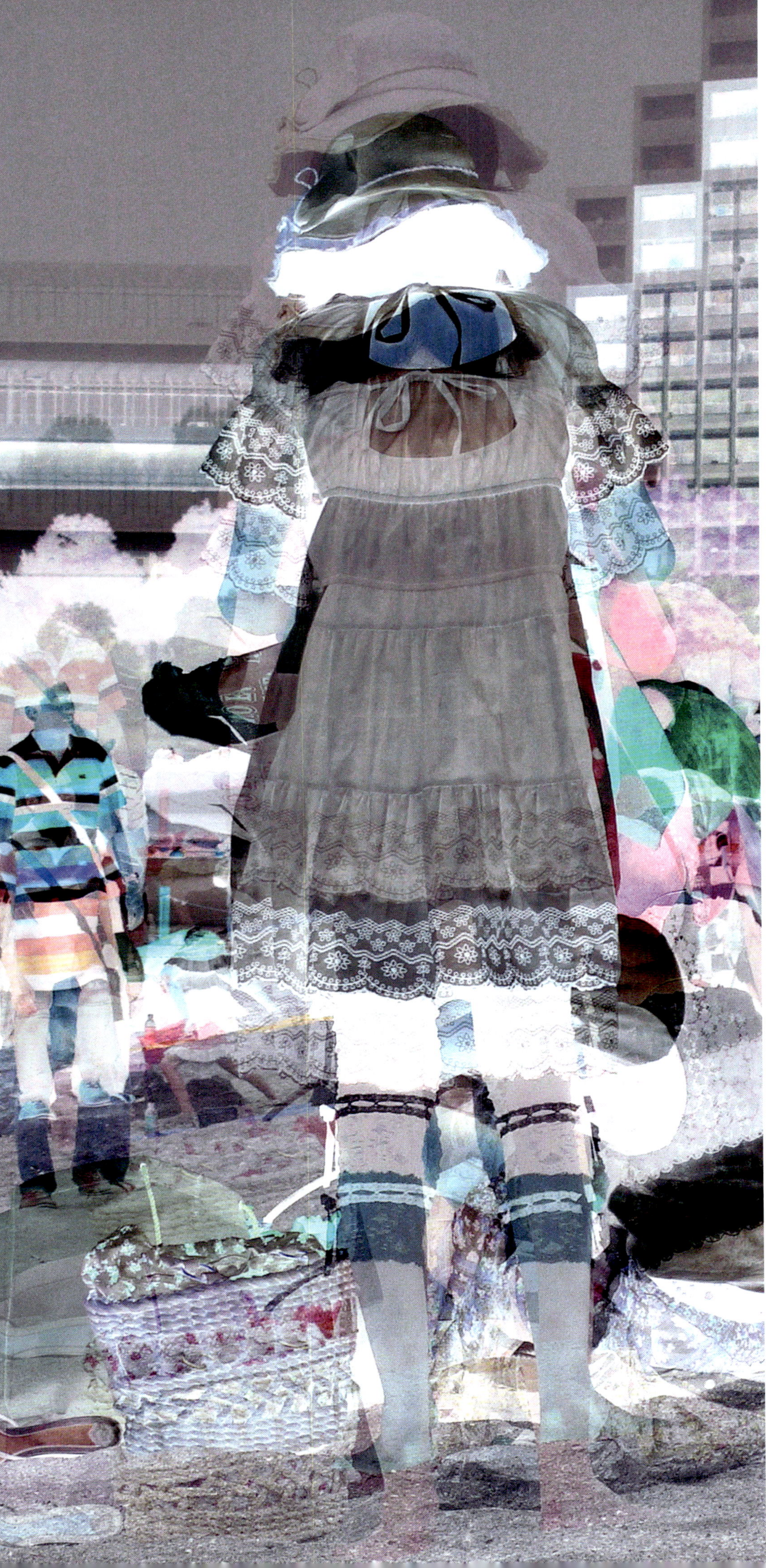

Tokyo Beach Duo / Tokyo / 2008

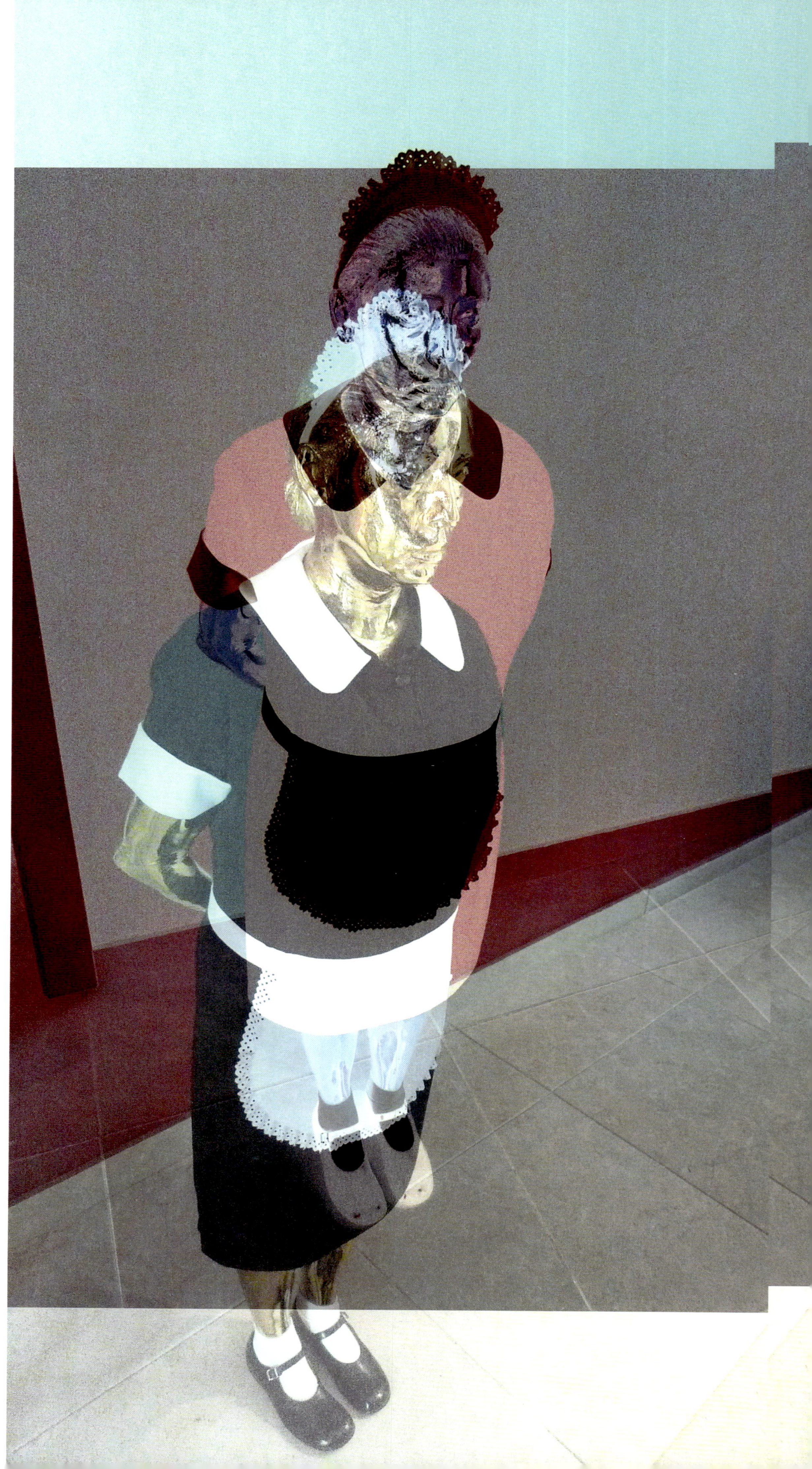

Lost in Venezia / Venice / 2008

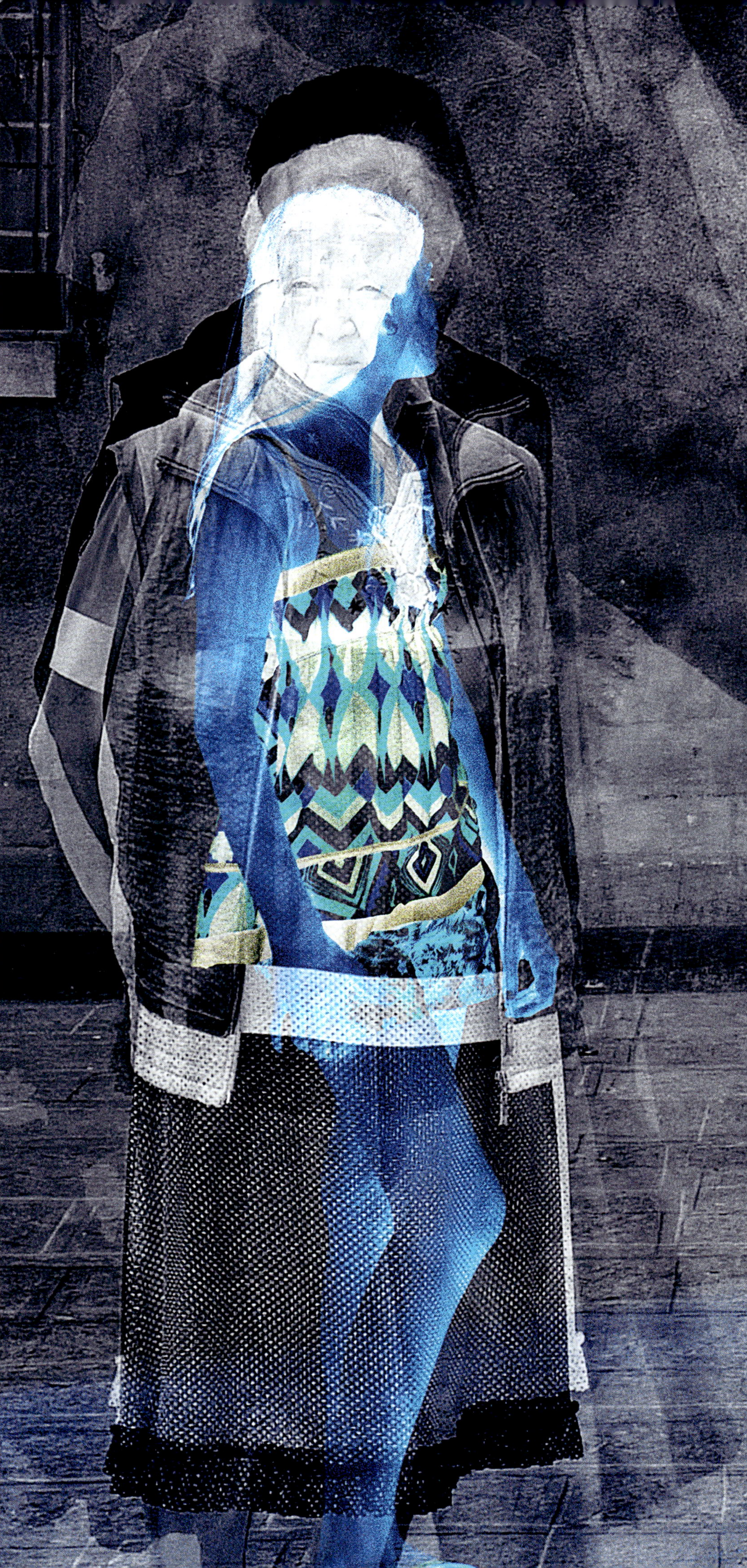

Burano Age / Burano / 2008

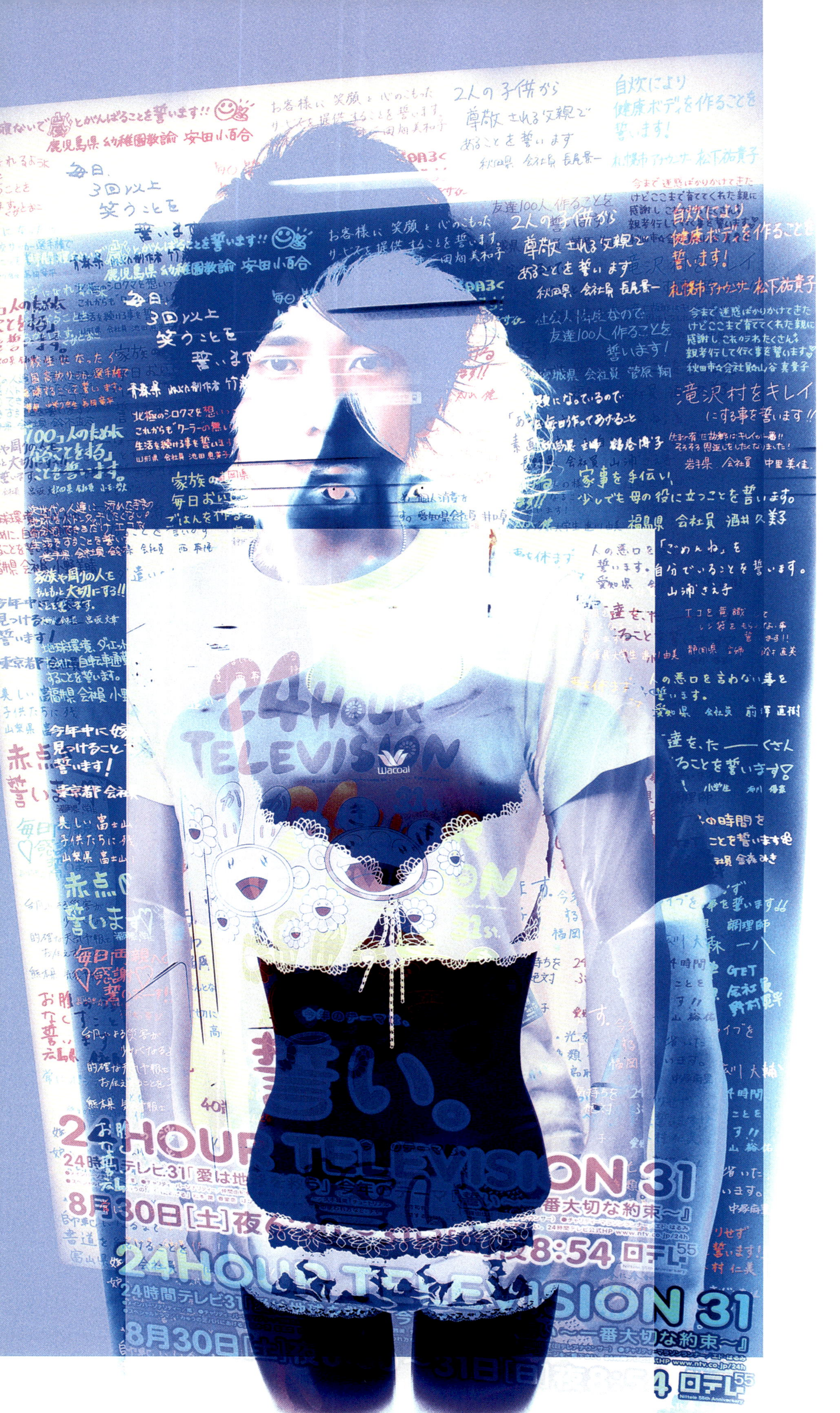

Tokyo Girl Inverted Blue / Tokyo / 2008

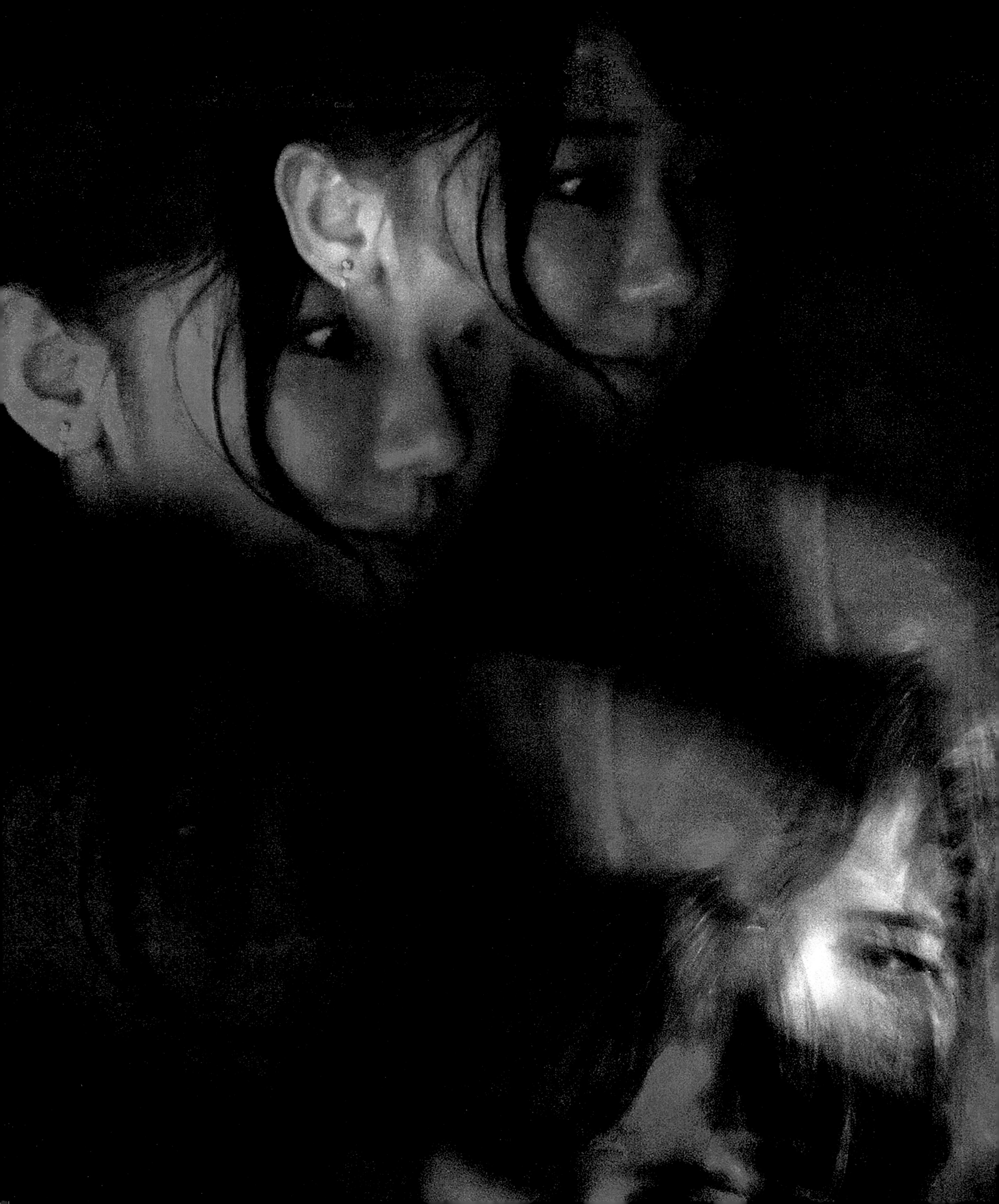

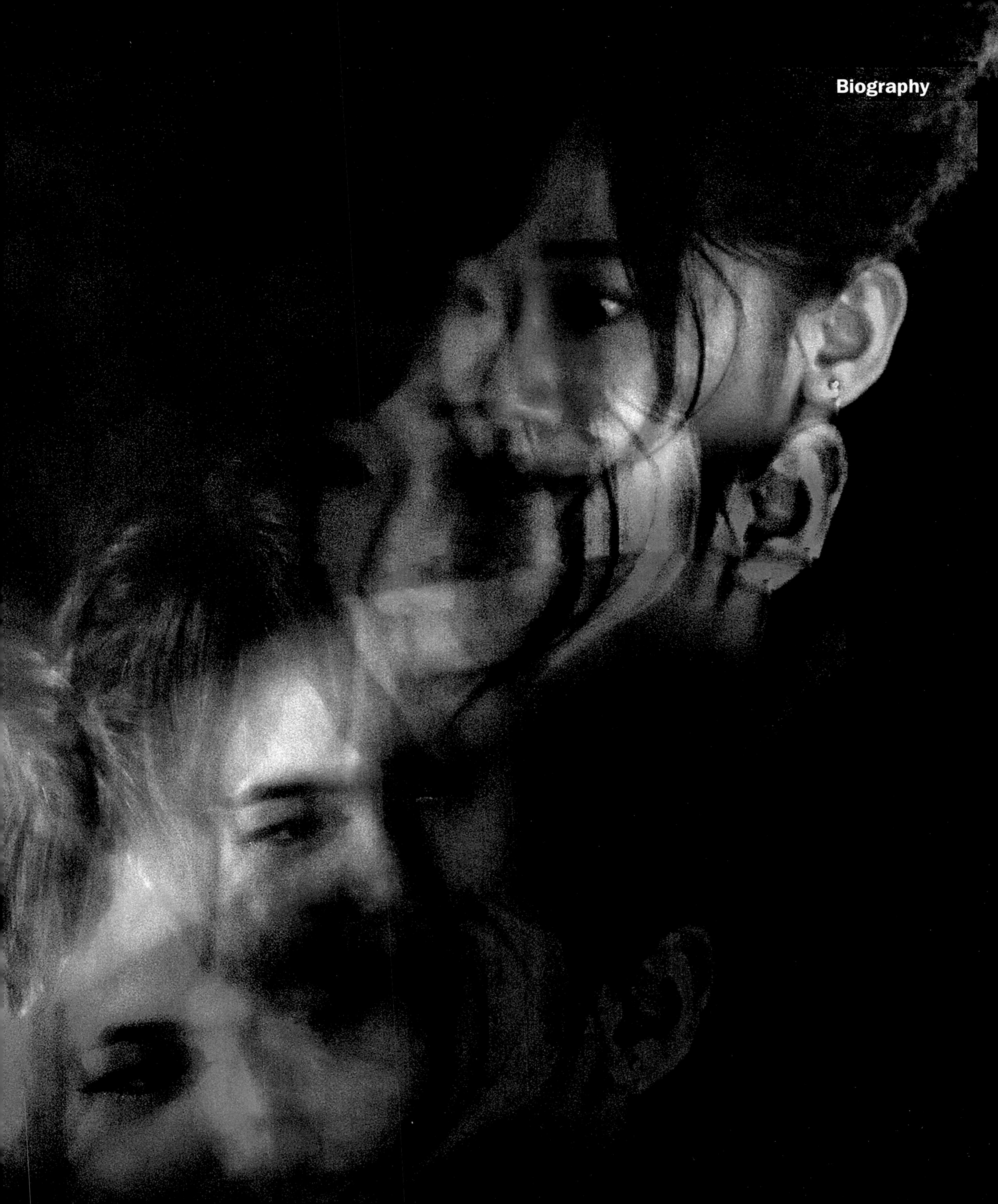

Klaus Mitteldorf was born in São Paulo on June 23, 1953. He began experimenting with photography when he was twelve years old, after his father gave him his first camera, a Yashica Mimi.

Starting in 1974, he began to document surfers on the beaches in São Paulo and Rio de Janeiro. His first photos and magazine cover were published in Rio de Janeiro by *Brasil Surf* magazine in 1975. That same year he also produced his first documentary film in Super 8 on surfing entitled *Terral*, the first of its kind in Brazil. In 1979, he graduated from the Braz Cubas University of Architecture and Urban Planning in Mogi das Cruzes.

In the early 1980s, Mitteldorf set up his studio in São Paulo, where he produced photographic campaigns for major ad agencies for over twenty years, including work for clients in Germany, where he lived from 1988 to 1996. His portfolio of clients in Brazil include the advertising agencies DPZ, Neogama, DM9, Africa, W Brasil, Talent, J. Walter Thompson, Young & Rubicam, McCann, ALMAP BBDO, Ogilvy, Lintas, Lowe Worldwide. His international clients include Young & Rubicam Frankfurt, BBDO Hamburg, McCann Frankfurt, and J. Walter Thompson New York.

His photographic work has been published in magazines such as *Vogue*, *Elle* (Brazil, Germany), *Playboy* (Germany, the United States, and Brazil) *Photo France*, *Zoom France*, *Graphis* (New York), and many other magazines specializing in art and photography.

In 2001, he was the first to win the Conrado Wessel Foundation Photography Award in São Paulo. In 2008, he won the Overseas Prize at the International Photography Festival in Higashikawa, Japan, for the photos in his book *O Último Grito / The Last Cry*, which was also exhibited at the Pinacoteca do Estado de São Paulo in 1998.

Mitteldorf has published ten books in Brazil, Germany, the United States, and Switzerland, and has had numerous international solo exhibitions. He lives and works in São Paulo and is involved in the production of two fiction feature films, *Rio-Santos* and *Cans On The Beach*.

Selected Solo Exhibitions
2013
Work, Klaus Mitteldorf 1983–2013, Museu de Arte
Brasiliera, Fundação Armando Alvares Penteado,
São Paulo, Brazil

2011
São Paulo Blues, Museu da Imagem e do Som,
São Paulo, Brazil

2008
Cries and Visions, Higashikawa International Photo
Festival, Higashikawa, Japan

2007
Introvisão, Pinacoteca do Estado de São Paulo, Brazil

2001
Katharsis, Estação Clínicas do Mêtro, Mês
Internacional de Fotografia, São Paulo, Brazil

1998–2000
O Último Grito, Pinacoteca do Estado de São Paulo.
Traveled to Museu Metropolitano de Arte de
Curitiba and Galeria dos Arcos, Porto Alegre, Brazil

1995
Divas, Museu Brasileiro da Escultura, São Paulo, Brazil

1992–93
Klaus Mitteldorf Photographs, Casa de Fotografia
Fuji, São Paulo, Brazil. Traveled to Fundação
Prometheus Libertus, Florianópolis, Brazil

1989
Norami, Galeria São Paulo, São Paulo, Brazil

1982
Galeria Itaú Higienópolis, São Paulo, Brazil

1981
Fiorucci Gallery, Rio de Janeiro and Salvador, Brazil

Selected Group Exhibitions
2014
Mostra São Paulo de Fotografia 2014, DOC Galeria,
São Paulo, Brazil

2013
O Mais Parecido Possível, O Retrato, Pinacoteca do
Estado de São Paulo, Brazil

2011
Galeria Nova Mafra, Belo Horizonte, Brazil
Focus Nu, Galeria Adler, Paris, France

2010
Tina Zappoli Galeria, Porto Alegre, Brazil

2008
Biennale d'Arte Internazionale di Roma, Rome, Italy

2007
Fotografia em Perspectiva, Museu de Arte Moderna de
São Paulo, Brazil

2004
Olho Vivo: A Arte da Fotografia, Acervo MAM São Paulo,
Santander Cultural, Porto Alegre, Brazil
São Paulo 450 Anos em 24 Horas, Instituto Cultural da
Caixa Econômica do Estado de São Paulo, Brazil
El Raptode la Luz, Instituto Cervantes de Bruselas,
Brussels, Belgium

2002
Surf Culture: The Art History of Surfing, Laguna Art
Museum, Laguna Beach, California

1999
A Imagem do Som de Chico Buarque, Paço Imperial,
Rio de Janeiro, Brazil

1998
A Imagem do Som de Caetano Veloso, Paço Imperial,
Rio de Janeiro, Brazil

1996
Die Farbe Blau, Airport Gallery, Frankfurt International
Airport, Frankfurt, Germany

1993
*Ano 2: Klaus Mitteldorf, Aguilar, Arnaldo Antunes e
Angeli*, Espaço Cultural Ovidio, São Paulo, Brazil

1992
2o Plak-Art, Galerie Rahmel, Cologne, Germany

1991
Bilderlust, Museum Ludwig, Cologne, Germany

1998
Kodachrome Classics, Photokina, Cologne, Germany

1985
Primiera Quadrienal de Fotografia, Museu de Arte
Moderna de São Paulo, Brazil

Permanent Collections
Itaú Cultural, São Paulo, Brazil
Coleção Pirelli, Museu de Arte de São Paulo, Brazil
Deutsche Fototage, Frankfurt, Germany
Die Neue Sammlung, Staatliches Museum für
Angewandte Kunst, Munich, Germany
Fotomuseum, Frankfurt, Germany
Fundação Cultural de Curitiba, Curitiba, Brazil
Higashikawa Museum, Higashikawa, Japan
Museu de Arte Contemporânea de São Paulo, Brazil
Museu de Arte Brasileira, Fundaçao Armando Alvares
Penteado, São Paulo, Brazil
Museu de Arte Moderna de São Paulo, Brazil
Museu de Arte Contemporânea do Ceará, Fortaleza,
Brazil
Musée Française de la Photographie, Paris, France
Pinacoteca do Estado de São Paulo, Brazil
Sammlung Uwe Scheid, Cologne, Germany

Books
Coleção Senac de Fotografia / Klaus Mitteldorf.
São Paulo: Editora Senac, 2006.
Introvisão. São Paulo: Editora Cosac & Naify, 2006.
Katharsis. São Paulo: Editora DBA, 2001.
Klaus Mitteldorf / International Nude Photograph.
Munich: Verlag & Edition Gerhard Götze, 1995.
Klaus Mitteldorf Photographs. Frankfurt: ArtForum
Verlag, 1992.
Klaus Mitteldorf Work: Photographs 1983–2013.
Bologna: Damiani, 2013.
Mitteldorf, Klaus, David Carson, and Sidney Tenucci.
Almaquatica. São Paulo: Terra Virgem Editora,
2005.
Mitteldorf, Klaus and Sven Hoffman. *Mermaids*.
Berkeley, California: Gingko Press, 2005.
Norami, Klaus Mitteldorf Photographs. Mies,
Switzerland: Rotovision, and New York: Watson-
Guptill, 1989.
São Paulo Blues. São Paulo: Terra Virgem Editora,
2011.
O Último Grito / The Last Cry. São Paulo: Terra Virgem
Editora, 1998.

DAMIANI

Bologna, Italy
www.damianieditore.com
info@damianieditore.com

Design: Robin Brunelle, Matsumoto Incorporated, New York
Editorial Coordination: Amy Wilkins, Matsumoto Incorporated, New York
Copy Editor: Amy Wilkins, Matsumoto Incorporated, New York
Color separations, printing, and binding by Grafiche Damiani, Italy

Front cover: *Berlin Face*, Berlin, 2013
Front endpaper, recto: *Tokyo Girls Pink Duo Acid*, Tokyo, 2008
Front endpaper, verso: *Berlin Party Duo*, Berlin, 2014
Pages 8–9: *Tati Duo*, São Paulo, 2015
Pages 92–93: *Secret Party Duo*, Honolulu, 2014
Back endpaper, recto: *Medusa Duo Grey*, São Paulo, 2015
Back endpaper, verso: *Cabra Cega*, Lido, 2009
Back cover: *The Idol Duo*, Berlin, 2014

ISBN 978-88-6208-456-7

Published in conjunction with the exhibition *Next*, Museu de Arte Brasiliera, Fundação Armando Alvares Penteado, São Paulo, Brazil.

Museu de Arte Brasiliera, Fundação Armando Alvares Penteado
Rua Alagoas, 903
Higienópolis
São Paulo–SP, 01242-001
Brazil
faap.br/museu

Klaus Mitteldorf is represented by
Galeria Millan
Rua Fradique Coutinho, 1360
Pinheiros
São Paulo–SP, 05416-000
Brazil
Phone: 55 11 3031 6007
Email: galeria@galeriamillan.com.br
galeriamillan.com.br

Klaus Mitteldorf
Phone: 55 11 9824 460 75
Email: k@klausmitteldorf.com
klausmitteldorf.com
rio-santos.com

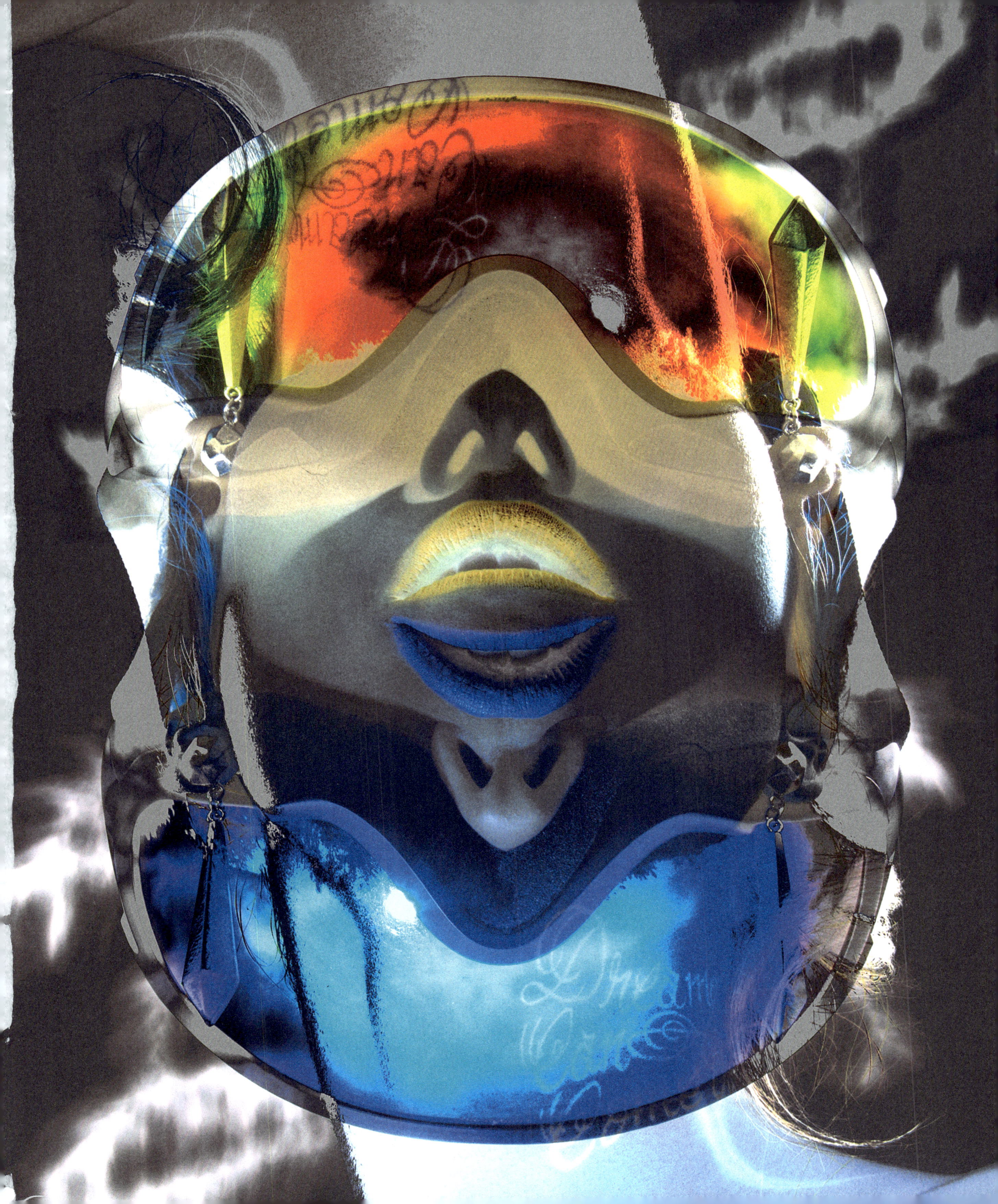

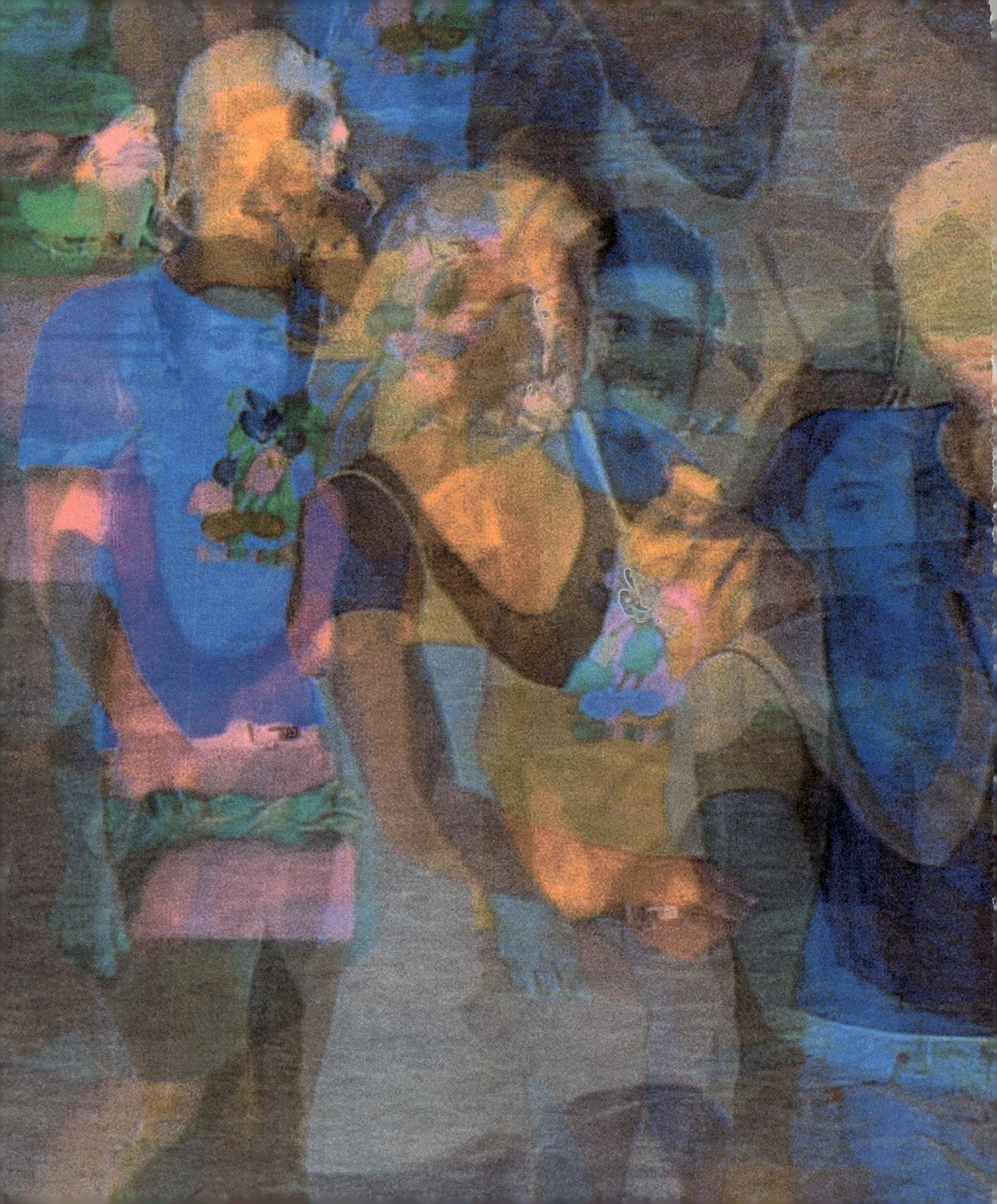